20 Canadian Poets
Take On the World

The Exile Book of
Poetry in Translation

20 Canadian Poets
Take On the World

edited by

Priscila Uppal

Exile Editions

Publishers of singular
Fiction, Poetry, Nonfiction, Drama, and Graphic Books
2009

Library and Archives Canada Cataloguing in Publication

The Exile book of poetry in translation : 20 Canadian poets take on the world / edited by Priscila Uppal.

ISBN 978-1-55096-122-5

I. Title.

PN6101.E99 2009   808.81   C2009-900966-8

Design and Composition by Active Design Haus
Typeset in Birka, Carlton and Garamond at the Moons of Jupiter Studios
Front cover photo © Duncan Walker/iStockphoto.com
Globe image (back cover and interior) © Stoupa/Dreamstime.com
Printed in Canada by Gauvin Imprimerie

The publisher would like to acknowledge the financial assistance of the
Canada Council for the Arts and the Ontario Arts Council, which is an agency
of the Government of Ontario.

Published in Canada in 2009 by Exile Editions Ltd.
144483 Southgate Road 14
General Delivery
Holstein, Ontario, N0G 2A0
info@exileeditions.com
www.ExileEditions.com

Canadian Sales Distribution: U.S. Sales Distribution:
McArthur & Company   Independent Publishers Group
c/o Harper Collins   814 North Franklin Street
1995 Markham Road   Chicago, IL 60610
Toronto, ON M1B 5M8   www.ipgbook.com
toll free: 1 800 387 0117   toll free: 1 800 888 4741

for Antonette di Paolo Healey, Branko Gorjup, & Richard Teleky,
for introducing me to the world of translation

&

for all those who seek the mot juste for a mot juste

CONTENTS

A Poet's Duty ~ An Introduction

A translator is an 'artist on oath.'
—A.K. RAMANUJAN

This anthology started taking shape as I was selecting poetry anthologies for my university courses, as I have always tried to expose my students not only to great English-language poets but also to great poets from around the world. It occurred to me while I was surveying these collections, such as *Scanning the Century* and *A Book of Luminous Things*, that most of the translations included, whether of major poets or unknown poets of major quality, were undertaken by major American and U.K. poets (W.H. Auden, Joseph Brodsky, Elizabeth Bishop, Carolyn Forché, Robert Hass, Seamus Heaney, Ted Hughes, Denise Levertov, Robert Lowell, Czesław Miłosz, Charles Simic, to name only a few). Yet, I noticed, in Canada, a country that prides itself on official bilingualism and multiculturalism, there is almost no translation tradition among our practising poets (and among our writers as a whole). What well-known Canadian poet could I name who was an active translator to boot – a poet with several collections as well as several books of translated verse? Very few. Barry Callaghan and Erín Moure came immediately to mind. Then David Soloway and Robert Majzels. And then I had to reach into the past to dredge up more names: John Glassco, F.R. Scott (called "Canada's first artistic translator of poetry" by Glassco), Louis Fréchette.

In discussing a citizen's responsibilities, in an introduction to a 1963 Canadian-Hungarian anthology, *The Plough and the Pen*, W.H. Auden wrote that a writer's only political duty "is a duty to translate the fiction and poetry of other countries so as to make them available to readers in his own." Do the few names above represent the only Canadian poets who have welcomed this poet's duty? Of course not. There have been others. And there are others (Roo Borson, Robert Bringhurst, Anne Carson, John Robert Colombo, Beatriz Hausner, Daniel Sloate, Ewan Whyte, and more, as well as many poets included here). I'm not trying in any way to minimize the importance of the work that has already been done, but I'm still unconvinced as to whether the Canadian poetry community has effectively countered Philip Stratford's assertion in his *Bibliography of Canadian Books in Translation*, published in 1977, that "Canada has as yet no tradition in literary translation." Stratford was looking at the translation of French to English and vice versa within Canada; the results of international translation were even weaker. As noted translator and past President of the Literary Translators' Association of Canada, Ray Ellenwood pointed out when reviewing the available European statistics for the early 70s, "A score of 949 for Denmark against 9 for Team Translation Canadian cannot be ignored."

Hearing Auden's dictum in the back of my mind as I picked my course texts, I certainly had to admit I had ignored it. Even a vague concept of "a poet's duty" causes one to reevaluate whether or not, as a poet, one is contributing to a growing understanding, appreciation, and awareness of literature, beyond one's own work. If not, why not? Why do so few Canadian poets translate the works of other poets? And shouldn't I hang my head, rather sheepishly, since I have (until now) only published a single translated poem – a very liberal post-9/11 rendering of the Anglo-Saxon elegy "The Wanderer" in my 2006 collection *Ontological Necessities*?

But translation is not an easy endeavour, and the creation of a tradition of literary translation is even more difficult to undertake. I would argue that translation is not a process generally cultivated and supported in our poetry communities, or in our wider literary communities. Translators are usually paid by the word, so the going rate for poetry – a minimalist genre in terms of word count, but one of the most difficult in terms of linguistic exertion – is quite low. Although some awards and grants recognizing and supporting translation do exist, these are few and far between, and therefore barely acknowledge, let alone encourage, Canadians to produce literary translations. Yet here we are, probably the most multicultural country in the world, at a time in global history where access to information about other cultures and our ability to encounter and engage with other cultures and languages is at an all-time high.

Hopefully, I thought, as I pondered my lack of translation experience, this will change. Literary translation in Canada has evolved and will continue to evolve due to dedicated individuals as well as organizations. I wished to contribute to this growth by proposing a collective project, a space where one could find a community of talented poets translating other talented poets across languages, across borders, across oceans, across time. I wanted a few poets who were already accomplished translators, and a few who had translated now and again, but also invited prominent and emerging poets to try their hand at translating for the first time, or even to translate from a language completely foreign to them (with help from others who could provide transliteral versions of the poems). Furthermore, I wanted to include the original works, those foreign accents and scripts and sounds, alongside the translations.

My experience of poets is that they are indeed generous people when an idea, passion, or interest grips them, and so I wondered if all these poets would be willing to each produce a handful of translations for this project, and if we could donate all profits (each of the poets have worked *pro bono* on this project and permissions fees were also generously waived, for which I am very grateful) to fund full-length collections of poetry in English translation not currently supported by the granting councils. Exile was a natural publisher in this regard, as it has been one of the few Canadian presses to regularly publish complete works in translation (and not just French to English) for over 30 years, both in its magazine, *Exile: The Literary Quarterly,* and through the publishing house, Exile Editions. The list is impressive and extensive, and because of Exile's publications I have encountered many great poets from across Europe and Latin America that I wouldn't have otherwise known. (I have also included appendices listing all the translations – poetry and prose – which Exile Editions and *Exile: The Literary Quarterly* have published, at the end of this book, a resource that I hope will be useful to readers and writers alike.)

The enthusiastic support for the project was overwhelming. When the selections started to come in, I was very pleasantly surprised by how accomplished and varied the translations were in terms of language (there are over a dozen languages represented in this anthology), but also in terms of voice, tone, subject matter, aesthetics, and, not least, how varied the translation process itself was from poet to poet. Each was asked to also provide a short introduction to their contribution that would either speak to why this particular poet had been chosen, or delve into some of the beauties and challenges of the translation process itself. The intention was to create a dialogue around translation that carried throughout the book between the poems, and which might be a useful teaching tool and resource for our future translators, and for translation exercises in creative writing or literature courses. In addition, these statements continually reengage the reader with the translation process as well as dialogues and debates surrounding translation itself – a rich literary tradition in its own right from Cicero to John Dryden to Ezra Pound to Walter Benjamin to our own Barbara Godard.

Translation has been alternately described as a "bearing across," a "smuggling," a "bastard art," a "hybrid form," "an art," "a gift." Although many critics have pointed out that translation has no official muse, it has certainly elicited a great deal of musings on the nature of language, communication, and the creation of meaning. Translators, and translating poets in particular, face many challenges as they aim, as "artists under oath," to render the original text in new form. Every word choice must be weighed for semantic meaning, tone, philosophy, emotional resonance, historical context, idiom, sound, rhythm, syllabic count, image patterning, as well as a dozen other considerations, many of which can barely be articulated in language. What stance is the poet to take? What are the qualifications of a translator? What *is* translation?

Constance Garnett argues in "The Art of Translation": "The qualifications for a translator are to be in sympathy with the author he is translating, and most important of all to be in love with words and interested in all their meanings. The language of a country is the soul of its people, and if you debase the language you debase the people and rob them of their language." Robert Lowell in his preface to *Imitations*: "I believe that poetic translation – I would call it imitation – must be expert and inspired, and needs at least as much technique, luck and rightness of hand as an original poem." Gayatri Chakravorty Spivak in her "Translator's Preface" to Jacques Derrida's *Of Grammatology*: "Translation is the most intimate act of reading. Unless the translator has earned the right to become the intimate reader, she cannot surrender to the text, cannot respond to the special call of the text." And the best articulation of the poet's dilemma at every word choice is perhaps uttered by Gregory Rabassa in "If This Be Treason: Translation and Its Possibilities," that the translator "must find the *mot juste* for a *mot juste* out of his own bag of possibilities in a different language." These are only a few notable responses to the above questions, but it does make one aware of how great the poet's duty really is, and why many would, with reason, avoid or decline the challenge.

Furthermore, a poet's duty can extend beyond the act of translation, to the nature of communication itself. In "The Task of the Translator," perhaps the most famous piece written on the art of translation, Walter Benjamin argues against old discussions of fidelity and license, towards a theory of pure language:

> Unlike a work of literature, translation does not find itself in the center of the language forest but on the outside facing the wooded ridge; it calls into it without entering, aiming at that single spot where the echo is able to give, in its own language, the reverbertation of the work in the alien one. Not only does the aim of translation differ from that of a literary work – it intends language as a whole, taking an individual work in an alien language as a point of departure – but it is a different effort altogether. The intention of the poet is spontaneous, primary, graphic; that of the translator is derivative, ultimate, ideational. For the great motif of integrating many tongues into one true language is at work.

And George Steiner in *After Babel*, claims: "Language is the main instrument of man's refusal to accept the world as it is." Therefore, when he writes, "inside or between languages, human communication equals translation," one can't help but see translation as an extremely important instrument of connection between nations, literatures, and peoples.

Poets, as our language-changers and language-protectors, are in a privileged position as translators, with talents, insights, and inspirations that are sometimes vastly different from academic or professional translators. Their translations can frequently move beyond literal translations of semantic meaning into recreations, often because they will not shy away from experimental or unconventional approaches to the act of transforming language. It is often fruitful and enlightening to read several versions of the same poem translated by different hands and to note the alternatives and decisions made. We need more translation from many circles, but in Canada, we especially need more translation from our poets. Not only would such a collective initiative introduce us to previously inaccessible poets and literatures, or to new experiences of available poets and literatures, but I think it would inspire, challenge, and push our own poetics to new heights and into previously uncharted territories, thereby actively transforming our literature. As Daniel Weissbort attests, in "Editing *Modern Poetry in Translation*" (a U.K. journal he co-founded with Ted Hughes in 1966), the publishing and reading of works in other languages and from other nations was "a liberating experience," and enabled English poets to become aware of "new *possibilities* in poetry."

The poets herein offer their additions to translation history in Canada, and to this vital form of literary history, criticism, and production. Herein you will encounter Dutch, English, French, Galician, German, Greek, Hungarian, Korean, Latin, Polish, Portuguese, Romanian, Russian, Spanish, and even QR Code. You will visit eastern and western Europe,

South America, North America, Asia and the Mediterranean. You will find classical poets like Horace alongside very contemporary poets like Jan-Willem Anker. Male poets translated by female poets, and a female poet translated by a male poet. Poets who worked solitarily on their pieces, and others who worked collaboratively. And as many approaches to the act of translating as there are translators. For some, this was a whirlwind adventure, while others have been translating the same poet or poems for years, even decades.

Ezra Pound posited: "A great age of literature is perhaps always a great age of translations; or follows it." To take on the world is an invitation to explore and expand our current boundaries. My hope is that readers and writers alike will find themselves delving deeper into all the poets' works included here and perhaps become inspired to seek out other translated works or start translating as well. This book is a tip of the hat to all those past and present poets, scholars, and literary experts, who have taken on a poet's duty, and it lays out a red carpet to those of you who would like to join them.

Priscila Uppal
Toronto, 2009

Oana Avasilichioaei
translates Nichita Stănescu (Romanian)

Out of the vortex

"I am nothing but/ a stain of blood/ that talks," wrote Nichita Stănescu in 1978 in a poem entitled "Self-portrait" (*Occupational Sickness*). Considered "a people's poet" both in Romania and in Eastern Europe, Stănescu was popular but also populated by the many histories and vocabularies of those landscapes. I was driven to translate his work because his diction is complex and philosophical, inventive, impossible and full of neologisms, but also a "village" diction, full of dialects, folk tales and the raw, unmediated existence of the human. And to be able to translate, I had to embody my own *stain of blood* and do my own talking in English.

Avidly writing and publishing throughout the communist years, a time where any public text was highly censored and nationalized, Stănescu went to poetry for solace but also in disguise. This at times gives his texts symbolic or coded levels of meaning. For example, when taking up issues of war, conflict or the realities of a soldier, his soldier is often a medieval one fighting a pre-modern war. Many of his invented words, such as "cerbos" which he derived from "cerb" (a stag or male-deer) and which I transposed in "Elegy ten" as "antlered," come from the natural world and not from other levels of society, such as industry. Thus his poetry, while not particularly nationalistic, appears on the surface to remain neutral on aspects of contemporary communist times (which made it publishable), and yet carries an underlying critique of those times, representing many of the anxieties, ideas, hopes, questions and belief systems of its people.

The poems here come from a collection published in 1966, entitled *11 Elegii* (*11 Elegies*). To translate these elegies I had to invent, collide and leap so that the English could embody the dexterity of Stănescu's language and its rhythmic play, which becomes increasingly complex through the intense repetition of sense and rhythm. The elegies are vortexes, pulling me in with the tornado-strength of their language, into which I go willingly, only to find the peaceful calm of their centres. Out of such centres could I then write and whirl them anew.

Elegia a doua, Getica

lui Vasile Pârvan

În fiecare scorbură era aşezat un zeu.

Dacă se crăpa o piatră, repede era adus
şi pus acolo un zeu.

Era de ajuns să se rupă un pod,
ca să se aşeze în locul gol un zeu,

ori, pe şosele, s-apară în asfalt o groapă,
ca să se aşeze în ea un zeu.

O, nu te tăia la mână sau la picior,
din greşeală sau dinadins.

De îndată vor pune în rană un zeu,
ca peste tot, ca pretutindeni,
vor aşeza acolo un zeu
ca să ne-nchinăm lui, pentru că el
apără tot ceea ce se desparte de sine.

Ai grijă, luptătorule, nu-ţi pierde
ochiul,
pentru că vor aduce şi-ţi vor aşeza
în orbită un zeu
şi el va sta acolo, împietrit, iar noi
ne vom mişca sufletele slăvindu-l...
Şi chiar şi tu îţi vei urni sufletul
slăvindu-l ca pe străini.

Getic elegy, two

*for Vasile Pârvan**

In every tree hollow sat a god.

If a stone cracked, quick, they brought
and stuck a god there.

A footbridge had but to break,
for a god to sit in the emptied space,

or, on roads, a pothole to appear in the asphalt
for a god to sit in it.

Oh, don't slit your wrist or ankle
on purpose or by accident.

Instantly they'll stick a god in the wound,
as in every nook, everywhere,
they'll sit a god there
for us to pray to, since he
protects all that splits off from the self.

Take care, warrior, don't lose
your eye,
because they'll bring and stick
a god in the socket
and he'll stay there, stone-still, and we
will stir our souls worshipping him...
Even you will rouse your soul
worshipping him like you worship strangers.

---

* Vasile Pârvan (1882-1927) was a Romanian historian and archeologist.
In 1926 he wrote *Getica*, a historical-archeological work on the Dacians
(Getae), the ancient inhabitants of present-day Romania.

A cincea elegie
Tentaţia realului

N-am fost supărat niciodată pe mere
că sunt mere, pe frunze că sunt frunze,
pe umbră că e umbră, pe păsări că sunt păsări.
Dar merele, frunzele, umbrele, păsările
s-au supărat deodată pe mine.
Iată-mă dus la tribunalul frunzelor,
la tribunalul umbrelor, merelor, păsărilor,
tribunale rotunde, tribunale aeriene,
tribunale subţiri, răcoroase.
Iată-mă condamnat pentru neştiinţa,
pentru plictiseală, pentru nelinişte,
pentru nemişcare.
Sentinţe scrise în limba sâmburilor.
Acte de acuzare parafate
cu măruntaie de pasăre,
răcoroase penitenţe gri, hotărâte mie.
Stau în picioare, cu capul descoperit,
încerc să descifrez ceea ce mi se cuvine
pentru ignoranţa...
şi nu pot, nu pot să descifrez
nimic,
şi-această stare de spirit, ea însăşi,
se supără pe mine
şi mă condamnă, indescifrabil,
la o perpetuă aşteptare,
la o încordare a înţelesurilor în ele însele
până iau forma merelor, frunzelor,
umbrelor,
păsărilor.

Fifth elegy

Real's allure

I've never been mad at apples
for being apples, leaves for being leaves,
a shadow for being a shadow, birds for being birds.
But the apples, leaves, shadows, birds
suddenly get mad at me.
Look, I'm taken to the law courts of leaves,
law courts of shadows, apples, birds,
circular courts, aerial courts,
courts narrow and fresh.
Look, I'm convicted of ignorance,
of boredom, of anxiousness,
of stillness.
Sentences written in the seeds' tongue.
Charges initialed
with birds' entrails,
fresh grey penances, determined as mine.
I stand, with my head uncovered,
try to decipher what I deserve
for ignorance...
and I can't, can't decipher
anything,
and this state of being, the very one,
gets mad at me
and condemns me, indecipherably,
to a perpetual waiting,
to a straining of meanings within themselves
until I take the shape of apples, leaves
shadows,
birds.

Elegia a zecea
Sunt

Sunt bolnav. Mă doare o rană
călcată-n copite de cai fugind.
Invizibilul organ,
cel fără nume fiind,
neauzul, nevăzul,
nemirosul, negustul, nepipăitul
cel dintre ochi și timpan,
cel dintre deget și limbă,—
cu seara mi-a dispărut simultan.
Vine vederea, mai întăi, apoi pauză,
nu există ochi pentru ce vine;
vine mirosul, apoi liniște,
nu exista nări pentru ce vine;
apoi gustul, vibrația umedă,
apoi iarăși lipsă,
apoi timpanele pentru leneșele
mișcări de eclipsă;
apoi pipăitul, mângâiatul, alunecare
pe o ondulă întinsă,
iarnă-nghețată-a mișcărilor
mereu cu suprafața ninsă.
Dar eu sunt bolnav. Sunt bolnav
de ceva între auz și vedere,
de un fel de ochi, un fel de ureche
neinventată de ere.
Trupul ramură fără frunze,
trupul cerbos
rărindu-se-n spațiul liber

Elegy ten

I am

I'm sick. Ache from a wound
trampled by hooves of hurried horses.
Invisible organ,
the nameless one being
nonhearing, nonseeing
nonsmelling, nontasting, nontouching
the one between the eye and eardrum,
the one between the finger and tongue,—
vanished together with the evening.
Sight comes first, then a pause,
there are no eyes for what comes;
smell comes, then quiet,
there are no nostrils for what comes;
then taste, that wet vibration,
then absence again,
then eardrums for the eclipse's
languid movements;
then the fumbling, caressing, sliding
on an even wave,
frozen winter of movements
always with its snowy surface.
But I'm sick. Sick
from something between hearing and sight,
from some kind of eye, some kind of ear
uninvented for ages.
Body, a leafless branch,
antlered body
thinning out in open space,

după legile numai de os,
neapărate mi-a lăsat
suave organele sferei
între văz și auz, între gust și miros
întinzând ziduri ale tăcerii.
Sunt bolnav de zid, de zid dărâmat
de ochi-timpan, de papilă-mirositoare.
M-au călcat aerian
abstractele animale,
fugind speriate de abstracți vânători
speriați de o foame abstractă,
burțile lor țipând i-au stârnit
dintr-o foame abstractă.
Și au trecut peste organul ne-nveșmântat
în carne și nervi, în timpan și retină,
și la voia vidului cosmic lăsat
și la voia divină.
Organ pieziș, organ întins,
organ ascuns în idei, ca razele umile
în sferă, ca osul numit
calcaneu în călcâiul al lui Achile
lovit de-o săgeată mortală; organ
fluturat în afară
de trupul strict marmorean
și obișnuit doar să moară.
Iată-mă, îmbolnăvit de-o rană
închipuită între Steaua Polară
și steaua Canopus și steaua Arcturus
și Casiopeea din cerul de seară.
Mor de-o rană ce n-a încăput
în trupul meu apt pentru răni

following only the laws of bone,
defenceless, it left
the sphere's gentle organs,
between sight and hearing, between taste and smell
laying out walls of silence.
I'm sick of the wall, ruined wall
of eye-eardrum, of smelling-papilla.
Ethereal, they stepped on me
the abstract animals,
spooked, running from the abstract hunters
frightened by an abstract hunger
their screaming stomachs stirring them
out of an abstract hunger.
And they passed the organ un-cloaked
in flesh and nerves, in eardrum and retina
left to the will of the cosmic void
left to divine will.
Crooked organ, stretched-out organ,
organ hidden in ideas, like humble rays
in the sphere, like the calcaneus bone
in Achilles' heel
struck by a mortal arrow; organ
brandished outside
the strictly marmoreal body
accustomed only to dying.
Look, I'm sick from a wound
imagined between the Polar Star
and Canopus and Arcturus
and Cassiopeia in the evening sky.
Dying from a wound that didn't fit
in my body capable of wounds

cheltuite-n cuvinte, dând vamă de raze
la vămi.
Iată-mă, stau întins peste pietre şi gem,
organele-s sfărâmate, maestrul,
ah, e nebun căci el suferă
de-ntreg universul.
Mă doare că mărul e măr,
sunt bolnav de sâmburi şi de pietre,
de patru roţi, de ploaia măruntă
de meteoriţi, de corturi, de pete.
Organul numit iarbă mi-a fost păscut de cai,
organul numit taur mi-a fost înjunghiat
de fulgerul toreador şi zigurat
pe care tu arenă-l ai.
Organul Nor mi s-a topit
în ploi torenţiale, repezi,
şi de organul Iarnă, întregindu-te,
mereu te lepezi.
Mă doare diavolul şi verbul,
mă doare cuprul, aliorul,
mă doare câinele, şi iepurele, cerbul,
copacul, scândura, decorul.
Centrul atomului mă doare,
şi coasta cea care mă ţine
îndepărtat prin limita trupească
de trupurile celelalte, şi divine.
Sunt bolnav. Mă doare o rană
pe care o port pe tavă
ca pe sfârşitul Sfântului Ioan
într-un dans de aprigă slavă.
Nu sufăr ceea ce nu se vede,

spent on words, paying a custom duty of rays
at customs.
Look, I lie over stones and moan,
organs crushed, the maestro
ah, he's mad, for his illness
is the whole universe.
I ache that the apple is apple,
I'm sick of seeds and stones,
of four wheels, of fine rain
of meteors, tents, stains.
The organ named grass was grazed by horses,
the organ named bull was stabbed
by the lightning toreador and ziggurat
in your arena.
The Cloud organ was dissolved
in quick, torrential rains
and of the Winter organ, in piecing the self together
you rid yourself, always.
The devil and verb ache me,
the copper and milkweed ache me,
the dog, rabbit, stag ache me
the tree, plank, the décor.
The atom's centre aches me,
and the rib that keeps me,
through the body's limit, far
from other, divine bodies.
I'm sick. Ache from a wound
that I hold on a tray
like St. John's ending
in a dance of bitter glory.
I don't suffer from what can't be seen,

ceea ce nu se aude, nu se gustă,
ceea ce nu se miroase, ceea ce nu încape
în increierarea îngustă,
scheletică a insului meu,
pus la vederile lumii celei simple,
nerăbdând alte morți decât morțile
inventate de ea, să se-ntâmple.
Sunt bolnav nu de cântece,
ci de ferestre sparte,
de numărul unu sunt bolnav,
că nu se mai poate împarte
la două țâțe, la două sprâncene,
la două urechi, la două călcâie,
la două picioare în alergare
neputând să rămâie.
Că nu se poate împarte la doi ochi,
la doi rătăcitori, la doi struguri,
la doi lei răgind, și la doi
martiri odihnindu-se pe ruguri.

can't be heard, can't be tasted,
can't be smelled, can't fit
in the narrow, skeletal
braining of my own creaturehood,
kept in sight of the simple folk
enduring only the deaths
invented by them to occur.
I'm not sick of songs,
but of broken windows,
of number one I am sick,
that it can no longer be shared
between two tits, two eyebrows,
two ears, two heels,
two legs unable
to keep running.
That it can no longer be shared between two eyes,
two wanderers, two grapes,
two roaring lions, and two
martyrs resting on the pyres.

KEN BABSTOCK

TRANSLATES JAN-WILLEM ANKER (Dutch)

(with assistance in the Dutch by Liedewij Hawke)

Jan-Willem Anker is a young poet from Amsterdam. When I met Jan-Willem in Rotterdam, at the poetry festival there, he was working for that festival; in programming, I think, and so may well have had a hand in my being invited that year. Call it payback, debt, cronyism, what do I care? He, at the time, had no book published, but was placing poems in magazines in Europe. We stayed in touch, if an email every two years could be called "in touch." Deciding to translate some of his poems was a happy accident; due in equal parts to his sending me books as they appeared, Priscila Uppal's invitation to contribute to this anthology, and my own curiosity. I'd liked Jan-Willem and hoped I'd uncover something interesting in his poems. It was a fishing trip, an unveiling, an encounter with the ghostly aspect of Anker that composes his poems. He's a quiet, angular sort of fellow who could be a pro tennis player or a doctor or a bicycle courier (the last time I saw him he was pedalling alongside a canal on his bike). He'd asked me very technical questions regarding my own work. He'd allowed that my reading style reminded him of that manipulated, droning, adenoidal voice at the beginning of Radiohead's song, "fitter, happier." He's funny in person, and I think I may be guilty of draining some of the weird, understated humour from poems like "Hungry Fish" and "Beard."

I was helped immeasurably by Liedewij Hawke, not just with the Dutch-to-English cribs, but with equally important cultural differences I could not have otherwise been aware of; space, privacy, quiet, neighbours. They appear in Anker's work in a way that reminded me, while writing, of the narrator of Joseph O'Neill's *Netherland*. My thanks to Liedewij, and to Jan-Willem for letting me warp these slightly, they're at a remove from the Dutch originals. I fled into the poems and, in certain lines, said them as me.

Blauw dat zilver knipoogt

Krekels zenden elektrisch gezoem
uit de bomen, vuilcontainers
puilen, zwerfkatten, mierenhoop.

Hoogspanningsmasten torenen uit
boven braakland en bungalows
agaven langs de weg gegroepeerd.

Later ben ik aan ze blauw dat
zilver knipoogt, gebronsd bootje
wolken trekken naar de horizon.

Mannen scheppen wier in een kar
water maakt vlechten in het zand
zout op de lijven van badgasten.

In de schemer vlokt het schuim
zee stuift op, stofwolk in licht
dat steeds naar achteren schuift.

De avond valt in dromen uiteen
kwallen spoelen voor mijn voeten
schrikbeelden van vloeibaar glas.

Wanneer het donker bovendrijft
bewegen nagels naar mijn huid
breken golven op het lege strand.

Blue signalling silver

High-frequency crickets transmit
from the tree line, waste bins
bulge, alley cats, an anthill.

The great hydro pylons striding
over dormant fields and bungalows
clustered agaves dress the roadside.

Seaside, later, blue
signalling silver, bronzed little skiff
clouds haul toward the horizon.

Men rake up a cartload of kelp
water plaits pressed sand
rime of salt on the bodies baking.

Sea froth dispersing to flakes in the dusk
upsurge of spume, like a dust cloud backlit
it keeps sliding away.

Evening collapses into dreams
jellyfish slur past in the shallows
phantoms of liquid glass.

As it gets dark
nails advance on my skin
a dull surf, the beach is blank.

Baard

Telkens groeien stoppels uit je sinaasappelhuid, dekt
een baard je tronie af, verwildert zonder dat je het merkt.
Buiten je om wikkelt zich iets af in jezelf.
Biologeert je.

Iemand vertelde je dat zijn vader het uniform van een gedode
stierenvechter had aangeschaft. De man waste de bloedvlekken
eruit, hees zijn zoon in het ding en zette hem zo op de foto.

Morgen is je hoofd een naaldbos, bedenk je dat er stallen
zijn waarin onrustig de vechtstieren slapen. De arena is donker,
verlaten nog.

Beard

Morning, noon, night, morning, the stubble pins through
your cellulitic jaw, a beard beards your mug and keeps
coming, runs wild despite you. A thing within you approaching
completion without you. Mesmeric.

Someone tells of his father buying a dead matador's uniform.
He'd washed out the bloodstains, helped his son into it, and
photographed him like that.

Your face will be pine forest by morning; picture stables in
Spain where fighting bulls loll in uneasy sleep. The arena
dark, deserted still.

Hungry Fish*

In de trein hangt de geur van insectenverdelger en je kent
het traject van buiten, weet wanneer bouwlampen
zijn verplaatst langs het spoor.

In je mobiel zwemt een goudvis, dat ben jij.
Vraatzuchtig groei je in etappes uit tot geel monster.
Zonder jou zou er vrede zijn in het spel.
Maar welk spel is vreedzaam?

Hoe dan ook verhonger je. Er in geen winnaar, geen tegenstander
om te verslaan. Alleen puntenwaardering. Jet doet het
goed of slecht—de enige die dat weet, ben je zelf.

---

* The title of the original poem is in English.

Hungry Fish

The smell of insecticide drifts through the train;
you know this section of branch line by heart, can tell when
the job-site lights have been shifted down track.

Inside your mobile swims a goldfish—the goldfish is you.
You're morphing greedily, by stages, into a yellow monster.
Without you in the game peace might obtain.
But what game is peaceful, exactly?

Whatever, you're famished. There is no winner, no opponent
to vanquish. Only a point score. You're showing well,
or not at all—who but you would know?

De toetseniste

Diep in de uitgestorven nacht rook je een muizenlijk. De geur
steeg op vanachter de koelkast waar het dier door honger of
elektrocutie omgekomen was. Je dacht aan de toetseniste die je
laatst zag spelen in een amateurband.

Het leek of ze dictaat opnam achter een lessenaar, notulen
maakte van een vergadering in muziek. Onduidelijk was de
relatie tussen het geluid dat ze voortbracht en de toetsen die ze
indrukte. Een toon ontsnapte eerder aan haar vingers dan aan
de synthesizer zelf.

Wanneer haar instrument overbodig was, verdween ze achter de
gordijnen. In de duisternis—een ruimte al een zondags pakhuis,
een donkere arena—wachtte ze tot ze weer opt mocht.

Ze miste nog dat een van de gitaristen uit baldadigheid zijn
gitaar in de bedrading boven hem hing, tot ongenoegen van de
geluidstechnicus die vanaf een hoger gelegen balkon luid begon
te protesteren.

Voor het slotnummer aanbrak, zonderde de toetseniste zich
weer af, om na afloop behoedzaam het podium op te stappen.
Ze troke een spits gezicht en zocht doodstil de felst verichte
hoek op in de zaal.

The Keyboardist

Deserted stillness past midnight; mouse carcass drifts up at
you on the kitchen air. The smell wafts out from behind the
fridge where the animal died of hunger, or chewed through
wiring. You think of the keyboardist you'd seen performing
in a band from around here.

Like she was taking dictation at a rolltop desk, writing up
the minutes from a meeting about music. The relation
between the tones produced and her fingerpads on the
synth's keys lost. Music emanating direct from her hands
rather than the machine's workings.

When not required to play she'd disappear back in the wings.
From that obscurity—a space like a Sunday warehouse, dark
arena—she'd wait for her cue to perform again.

Her bandmate—she'd missed this—had hung his guitar, for
kicks, from the overhead rigging. The sound guy hurled
protestations down from the balcony seats.

Before the closing number began, the keyboardist secluded
herself, as before, in the shroud of black curtain; then, again,
picked her way downstage after the gig. Her face cinched up,
drew to a point. Standing very still, she sought out a halo of
that hall's spot-lit space; it held her gaze.

In Het Zuiden

In de streekbus zie ik legerhelikopters gaan
parachutisten zakken als kwallen in de lucht
wiegen richting hun landingsgebied, later pas

een burcht in de lichtshow van de middag
stelletjes die zichzelf en elkaar fotograferen
mannen in leren jack, vriendinnen op pumps.

Kinderstemmen schieten van het basketbalplein
geluid van drilboren, claxons, bouwverkeer
een racemotor geeft gas bij het pompstation

uitzicht op de atletiekbaan, uitgestorven tribune
de pier waar vissersboten liggen aangemeerd
het forteiland, onbereikbare relikwie in de baai.

Aan de kade staat een sokkel zonder monument
bekrast met namen van mensen die ik niet ken
jaartallen waarbij ik aan andere oorden denk.

Op terrassen spelen jongens backgammon
meisjes met koffie frappé, trendy zonnebrillen
sfinxen die elkaar hun raadsels voorleggen

ingesnoerde parasols, ambiant uit de speakers
van het paviljoen waar grijsaards bijkomen
na een half uur schoolslag langs de boeien.

De wind steekt op, blaast mijn haar in de war
ik proef van de lucht, geur van zeevruchten
in een blinddoek van licht, adem van warmte.

In The South

From this milk-run bus I watch helicopters do a flyover
seeding the sky with paratroopers like jellyfish
that sway toward their drop point, only later

a citadel in afternoon's light show
couples photographing themselves, as couples and alone
men in leather jackets, their girlfriends in pumps.

Kids' voices flash from the basketball court
pneumatic drill, honking, clog of excavation trucks
a motorbike going full throttle. I can see

the athletics oval, its track and empty bleachers
the pier, its local fishing fleet tied in the slips
and the island fortress out in the bay, inaccessible relic.

On the quay sits a pedestal missing its monument
scratched with the names of people unknown to me
dates conjuring thoughts of other places.

Boys playing backgammon at sidewalk café tables
the girls with iced lattes, this year's sunglasses
sphinxes posing their riddles each to the other

cinched parasols, muzak from the pavilion
speakers where old men are recovering
after a half-hour breaststroke along the buoy-line.

The wind's getting up, ruffles my hair
I sip at the air and it's shot through with shellfish
light like a blindfold, gusts of sudden warmth.

De zee blinkt uit in haar verschijning
groen glijdt als waterverf in turquoise over
vervormt zacht gesmak tussen de rotsen.

Ooit zal de zon ondergaan achter een decor
van bergen, breedgeschouderd in de nevel
die het licht afvoert, geen vogel onthoudt.

White glare—the sea outshines the limits of itself
the deep green like water colour washes to turquoise
transforming soft slaps in among the rocks.

At some point the sun will sink behind a backdrop
of mountains, broad-shouldered in the mist
the birdless light draining away with it.

Overbuurvrouw

Ineens trekt de overbuurvrouw
vanachter de beschuttende muur

de rolgordijnen naar zich toe
schiet de siasmees naar voren

uit het duister van de kamer
een schaduw die niet beweegt

dan volgt zijzelf in ochtendjas
plaatst haar handen op de ruiten

vinger voor vinger voor vinger
alsof ze huisarrest heeft gekregen

laat zee en vette handschoen na
als ze zich wendt tot de poes

vormen haar lippen zich naar
de contouren van een woord

schampen toevallig onze blikken
zien we de leegte om ons heen.

The Neighbour Opposite

From behind the fence wall
suddenly the woman pulls

her blinds towards her
the Siamese darts forward

out of the darkness of the room
a shadow that doesn't move

then she herself follows in her housecoat
puts her hands on the windowpanes

finger by finger by finger
as if placed under house arrest

it leaves a greasy glove print
when she turns to the cat

her lips mold themselves to
the contours of a word

our glances meet, then deflect
then re-enter our quieter rooms.

CHRISTIAN BÖK

TRANSLATES ARTHUR RIMBAUD (French)

Notes to the Translations

Voyelles

Arthur Rimbaud is, of course, one of the most celebrated luminaries of Symbolist decadence, and his poetry constitutes one of the cornerstones of the avant-garde in the early 20th century. "Voyelles," his fabled sonnet about the "colours" of the vowels, offers a series of hallucinations about these emotional lynchpins of language.

Vowels

"Voyelles" is famously difficult to translate, and many English versions preserve its literal content at the expense of its musical quality. Rimbaud uses a formal rhyme scheme (abba baab ccd eed) with lines of variant lengths, while my version retains his rhyming patterns, but accents the rigouros, syllabic contours of the alexandrine line.

Voile (from Eunoia)

"Voyelles" is an important influence upon my univocal lipogram Eunoia—a text, whose addendum includes my poem "Voile," a kind of homophonic translation of the sonnet by Rimbaud. My version uses English words to imitate the phonetic sequence, but not the semantic meanings, of the French words. The two poems sound alike when read aloud.

AEIOU (The True Sonnet)

"AEIOU" literalizes the referent for the title "Voyelles" by removing everything in the poem that is not a vowel (including consonants, punctuation, and letterspaces), thereby reducing the work to its most fundamental constituent. I can almost imagine someone writing a new set of sonnets that might yet still retain this identical sequence of vowels.

Voyelles

A noir, E blanc, I rouge, U vert, O bleu: voyelles,
Je dirai quelque jour vos naissances latentes:
A, noir corset velu des mouches éclatantes
Qui bombinent autour des puanteurs cruelles,

Golfes d'ombre; E, candeurs des vapeurs et des tentes,
Lances des glaciers fiers, rois blancs, frissons d'ombelles;
I, pourpres, sang craché, rire des lèvres belles
Dans la colère ou les ivresses pénitentes;

U, cycles, vibrements divins des mers virides,
Paix des pâtis semés d'animaux, paix des rides
Que l'alchimie imprime aux grands fronts studieux;

O, suprême Clairon plein des strideurs étranges,
Silences traversés des [Mondes et des Anges]:
—O l'Oméga, rayon violet de [Ses] Yeux!

Vowels

A black, E white, I red, U green, O blue: the vowels.
I will tell thee, one day, of thy newborn portents:
A, the black velvet cuirass of flies whose essence
commingles, abuzz, around the cruellest of smells,

Wells of shadow; E, the whitewash of mists and tents,
glaives of icebergs, albino kings, frostbit fennels;
I, the bruises, the blood spat from lips of damsels
who must laugh in scorn or shame, both intoxicants;

U, the waves, divine vibratos of verdant seas,
pleasant meadows rich with venery, grins of ease
which alchemy grants the visages of the wise;

O, the supreme Trumpeter of our strange sonnet—
quietudes crossed by another [World and Spirit],
O, the Omega!—the violet raygun of [Her] Eyes....

Voile

for Arthur Rimbaud

Anywhere near blank rage
you veer, oblivial.

Jade array, calico azure
evanescent talents.

Unaware, corrosives flow
to my shackled hand.

Key bombing an auto tour
to paint her colour.

Gulfs of amber contours
evaporate the tint.

Linseed glass or oblong
freezing dumbbells.

Upper pressing cashiers
do deliver verbals.

Dance the clear, elusive
rinse of paintings.

Icicle fibre meant divine
daymares varied.

Pity paid to see my dynamo
poised to rid us.

Cool chimes, a primal green
for studios.

Spur my clear plan astride
a stranger.

Cylinders versus diamonds
a decision.

Hollow, my grey ovule does
decide you.

AEIOU *(The True Sonnet, by Arthur Rimbaud)*

AOIEAIOUEUEOEUOEE
EIAIUEUEOUOAIAEAEE
AOIOEEUEOUEEAAE
UIOIEAUOUEUAEUUEE

OEOEEAEUEAEUEEEE
AEEAIEIEOIAIOOEE
IOUEAAEIEEEEEE
AAOEEOUEIEEEIEE

UEIEEIIEEIIE
AIEAIEEAIAUAIEIE
UEAIIEIIEAUAOUIEU

OUEEAIOEIEIEUEAE
IEEAEEEOEEEAE
OOEAAOIOEEEEU

AEIOU *(The True Sonnet, by Christian Bök)*

AAEIEIEUEEOUEEOE
IIEEEOEAOEOOE
AEAEEUIAOIEOEEEE
OIEAUAOUEUEEOE

EOAOEEIEAOIAE
AIEOIEEAIOIOIEE
IEUIEEOOAOIOAE
OUAUIOOAEOIOIA

UEAEIIEIAOOEAEA
EAAEAOIIEEIOEAE
IAEAEIAEOEIE

OEUEEUEEOOUAEOE
UIEUEOEAOEOAII
OEOEAEIOEAUOEEE

DIONNE BRAND
TRANSLATES PABLO NERUDA (Spanish)

I loved Pablo Neruda the minute I saw him on the page. Sitting in a small room in Toronto a long time ago I discovered the out-lines of his face and his hand in his poem "Arte Poetica" in his *Residencia I*. It began, "Entre sombra y espacio..." and I was summoned. Meeting him made me regret leaving the study of Spanish behind at fourteen, but meeting him kept Spanish close to me and I promised myself to learn the language just to listen to Neruda well. For years I read him, my Spanish diction-ary for reference, along with my dear friend Filomena Carvalho who shared my passion for his work. She herself was fluent in Spanish and Portuguese so I would call her and ask, could he have meant this instead of that. And for over twenty years we've had a running conversation about Neruda's meanings. Some-times around the same line or poem. I was learning Spanish through reading Neruda, and, frankly, English too. By this last I mean his work intimated a more limber, hallucinatory approach to English. His gestures were so fluid, his orbit, emotional and political, so capacious, his linguistic and metaphoric pivots so startling.

Then in a cottage at Indian River, Nova Scotia, three years ago I was reading again his posthumously published volumes when I decided to find a tutor and seriously study the lan-guage. Returning to Toronto I did just that and find myself now in the even more fertile expanse of Neruda's work in Spanish. So, "Entre sombra y espacio..." that is, "Between shadow and space..." where every poet works, I attempt here to distill some of the essence of a few of his love sonnets. Neruda's work is so forceful that for me it insinuates an English self even as it goes about its Spanish intentions. I proffer these four sonnets, taken from his *100 Love Sonnets/Cien sonetos de amor*, one from each of the four sections (morning, afternoon, evening, night), with gratitude for his lessons in English. Thank you, also, to M.O. for his suggestions.

Mañana

XI

Tengo hambre de tu boca, de tu voz, de tu pelo
y por las calles voy sin nutrirme, callado,
no me sostiene el pan, el alba me dequicia,
busco el sonido líquido de tus pies en el día.

Estoy hambriento de tu risa resbalada,
de tus manos color de furioso granero,
tengo hambre de la pálida piedra de tus uñas,
quiero comer tu piel como una intacta almendra.

Quiero comer el rayo quemado en tu hermosura,
la nariz soberana del arrogante rostro,
quiero comer la sombra fugaz de tus pestañas

y hambriento vengo y voy olfateando el crepúsculo
buscándote, buscando tu corazón caliente
como un puma en la soledad de Quitratúe.

Morning

XI

I hunger for your mouth, your voice, your hair
and I go through the streets starving, silent,
bread does not sustain me, the dawn disquiets me,
I search the day for the liquid sound of your footsteps.

I hunger for your slippery laugh,
your hands the colour of a furious harvest,
I crave the pale stone of your fingernails,
I want to eat your skin like an untouched almond.

I want to eat the burnt ray of your beauty,
the sovereign silhouette of your arrogant look,
I want to eat the fleeting shadow of your eyelashes

and famished I come and go scenting twilight
searching for you, seeking your beating heart
like a puma in the barrens of Quitratue.

Mediodia

XLI

Desdichas del mes de enero cuando el indiferente
mediodía establece su escuación en el cielo,
un oro duro como el vino de una copa colmada
llena la tierra hasta sus límites azules.

Desdichas de este tiempo parecidas a uvas
pequeñas que agruparon verde amargo,
confusas, escondidas lágrimas de los días
hasta que la intemperie publicó sus racimos.

Sí, gérmens, dolores, todo lo que palpita
aterrado, a la luz crepitante de enero,
madurará, arderá como ardieron los frutos.

Divididos serán los pesares: el alma
dará un golpe de viento, y la morada
quedará limpia con el pan fresco en la mesa.

Afternoon

XLI

Misfortunes of January when the indifferent
afternoon establishes its equation in the sky,
a hard gold like wine in an overflowing glass
fills the earth to its blue limits.

Misfortunes of this season so like tiny grapes
that gather green bitterness,
confused, hidden tears of the days,
until the elements disclose their clusters.

Yes, seeds, griefs, everything that stirs
terrified, in the crackling light of January,
will ripen, will burn out as fruit burns out.

Sorrows will split, the soul
will breath a gasp of air, and our dwelling
will be cleansed with fresh bread on the table.

Tarde

LVIII

Entre los espadones de fierro literario
paso yo como un marinero remoto
que no conoce las esquinas y que canta
porque sí, porque cómo si no fuera por eso.

De los atormentados archipiélagos traje
mi acordeón con borrascas, rachas de lluvia loca,
y una costumbre lenta de cosas naturales:
ellas determinaron mi corazón silvestre.

Así cuando los dientes de la literatura
trataron de morder mis honrados talones,
yo pasé, sin saber, cantando con el viento

hacia los almacenes lluviosos de mi infancia,
hacia los bosques fríos del Sur indefinible,
hacia donde mi vida se llenó con tu aroma.

Evening

LVIII

Among the sabres of literary iron
I travel like a remote sailor
who does not know the street corners and who sings
because yes, if not for that what else is there.

From the tormented archipelagoes I brought
my stormy accordion, torrents of mad rain,
and the slow habit of natural things,
these defined my wild heart.

So when the small teeth of Literature
tried to bite my honest heels,
I passed by, unknowingly, singing with the wind

toward the rainy warehouses of my childhood,
toward the cold forests of the indefinable South,
toward where my life filled itself with your fragrance.

Noche

XCVII

Hay que volar en este tiempo, a dónde?
Sin alas, sin avión, volar sin duda:
ya los pasos pasaron sin remedio,
no elevaron los pies del pasajero.

Hay que volar a cada instante como
las águilas, las moscas y los días,
hay que vencer los ojos de Saturno
y establecer allí nuevas campanas.

Ya no bastan zapatos ni caminos,
ya no sirve la tierra a los errantes,
ya cruzaron la noche las racíes,

y tú aparecerás en otra estrella
determinadamente transitoria
convertida por fin en amapola.

Night

XCVII

One has to fly in these times, but where to?
Without wings, without an airplane, fly, without a doubt,
already footsteps have passed on without remedy,
they couldn't uplift the feet of the passenger.

One has to fly at every instant, like
the eagles, the houseflies and the days,
one has to conquer the eyes of Saturn
and set up new church bells there.

Already neither shoes nor pathways are enough,
already the earth is no use to vagrants,
already our origins have crossed in the night,

and you will appear on another planet
resolutely transient
transformed finally into euphoric flowers.

Nicole Brossard
translates Elisa Sampedrín* (English to French)

Notes on translation of excerpts from Little Theatres

I do not have much experience in translation though my fascination for the process, the one I fantasize around, as I did in my novel *Mauve Desert*, has no limit. Probably because it is about how meaning comes and goes, vanishes, takes root or ramifies in our life so we can go on and take pleasure or escape boredom in the voyage among landscapes of meaning. Landscapes being made of the current vocabulary that history, science and personal experience have designed for us to understand life and to pretend that it has a specific meaning.

All anecdotes about the experience of translation are worth telling but of course I will not indulge in them. Nevertheless I would say that translating is like entering a new space. Reading is one thing but reading with the intention of translating is like entering a white space with dots here and there that you will have to relate to each other. Like walking on stones in the middle of a river while feeling the forest around you, listening to the sounds, noticing the nuance of colours in the rocks, the change of light, and not falling.

I chose a poet whose work is already related to translation and who likes to reshape meaning in such a way that it will activate traces of other languages within the one chosen to write. For example in the poem "Theatre of the Hope of a Cebola," I could not help reading the Spanish "*no hay*" instead of the English "no hay."

In her poems, Moure uses repetition and for me repetition always displaces and renews meaning. In her case, it kept me

---

* Elisa Sampedrín is the polyheteronym of several writers; in these poems she inhabits Erín Moure.

wondering about the symbolic use of the word or the factual meaning of the word. And so a word like *corn* became an obsession. As well, I got caught by surprise when I read "the water rose..." or "corn's dichten" or "A little river and a big river."

Translating is about synchronizing metaphorically our five senses for the purpose of making a decision. Then making sure it is the best decision. For an instant, six months, ten years or a century.

Eight Little Theatres of the Cornices

Theatre of the Green Leira (Mandúa)

Is bad weather coming
how would we know
Is bad weather coming
call everyone

I am all alone cutting the grass or grain
cutting the wood I am alone
splitting it open carrying it to the crib
Call everyone, put the white table out in the yard
sharpen the knives the scythes
bring out the books now
sharpen the clock's knives too

where did we read any of this
my heart mad with beating
I might lie down here in this field before you come

call everyone
the flies are singing their hymnal hum hum ai ai
how would we know

the needles of the clock are cutting down the names of the hours

Huit petits théâtres de la Corniche

Théâtre du champ vert (Mandua)

Le mauvais temps vient-il
comment le saurions-nous
Le mauvais temps vient-il
appelle tout le monde

Je suis toute seule en tondant le gazon ou le grain
en coupant le bois je suis seule
à le fendre, à le ranger dans la remise
Appelle tout le monde, sort la table blanche dans la cour
aiguise les couteaux les faux
maintenant apporte les livres
aiguise les aiguilles de l'horloge aussi

où avons-nous déjà lu quelque chose comme ça
mon coeur bat fou
il se peut que je m'allonge ici dans ce champ avant ton arrivée

appelle tout le monde
les mouches chantent leur cantique hum hum ai ai
comment le saurions-nous

les aiguilles de l'horloge écourtent le nom des heures

Theatre of the Stone Chapel (Abades)

In one of its cornices are the two boots of a man
In one of the stone canzorros
If you listen you can hear him walk
His walk is stone and
his gasoline is stone
and his quill is stone

that's why he hasn't written
because his quill is stone

that's why he hasn't come yet
his gasoline is stone

that's why at night you hear him walking
his boots are stone

even his field of corn is stone
and his mother is water

Théâtre de la chapelle en pierre (Abades)

Sur une de ses corniches il y a les deux bottes d'un homme
Dans une des pierres *canzorros*
Si tu écoutes tu peux l'entendre marcher
Sa marche est de pierre et
son essence est de pierre
et sa plume est de pierre

c'est pourquoi il n'a pas écrit
car sa plume est de pierre

c'est pourquoi il n'est pas encore arrivé
son essence est de pierre

c'est pourquoi la nuit tu l'entends marcher
ses bottes sont de pierre

même son champ de maïs est de pierre
et sa mère c'est de l'eau

Theatre of the Hope of a Cebola (Santiso)

On the hill there is no hay
but rain

no hay for a hayrick but
small rivulets singing the grass down

An onion has toppled off a high cart
the chest of the high cart has gone on past the hill

if pressed with a shoe an onion toppled
may take root

Will a shoe ever find it
how can we know

will the onion find a mouth to eat it
how can we ever know

In the channels of water:
small blue rivulets of blue

Théâtre de l'espoir d'un oignon (Santiso)

Sur la colline il n'y a pas de foin
mais de la pluie

pas de foin pour une meule mais
ruisselets chantant dans l'herbe

Un oignon est tombé d'une charrette
le coffre de la charrette a continué au-delà de la colline

si un soulier l'écrase, un oignon renversé
peut s'enraciner

Y aura-t-il jamais un soulier pour le trouver
comment savoir

l'oignon rencontrera-t-il une bouche pour le manger
le saurons-nous jamais

Dans les canaux d'eau:
bleus ruisselets de bleu barbeau

Theatre of the Millo Seco (Botos)

I am in the little field of my mother
Her field touches
oaks of the valley
and I touch the faces of my corn

Opening corn's faces
so that my hands touch its braille letters
The face of corn is all in braille
the corn wrote it

Fires will burn this evening
burn the dry husks of the corn
and I will learn to read
Sheep will wait by the trough
for they know corn's feature, corn's humility

corn's dichten

grain's

granite too

Théâtre du maïs sec (Botos)

Je suis dans le petit champ de ma mère
Son champ touche
les chênes de la vallée
et je touche aux visages de mon histoire

Dénudant le maïs de sa gaine
afin que mes mains touchent ses lettres en braille
L'intérieur du maïs est tout en braille
l'épi l'a écrit

Des feux brûleront ce soir
la cosse sèche du maïs brûlera
et j'apprendrai à lire
Les moutons attendront près de la mangeoire
car ils connaissent les traits et l'humilité du maïs

la composition poétique du maïs

du grain

granite aussi

Theatre of the Peito (Santiso)

In a woman's arms lies a man
his skin is blue and his lips are blue
and his chest is a hayrick
flat with forks of blue
Perhaps he is dead, perhaps he is dreaming
perhaps he remembers the law has smote him down

he has shut his eyes
his eyes are open
his chest is a hayrick
His head is very tiny, bearded with a thread

his head has the breadth of an onion
in a mother's arms
where is she carrying this onion:
its chest is so huge!
on the road above the house roofs:

why is this onion passing by?

Théâtre de la poitrine (Santiso)

Un homme repose dans les bras d'une femme
sa peau est bleue et ses lèvres sont bleues
et sa poitrine est une meule
fauchée d'éclats de fourches en bleu
Peut-être est-il mort, peut-être rêve-t-il
peut-être se souvient-il que la loi l'a foudroyé

il a fermé ses yeux
ses yeux sont ouverts
sa poitrine est une meule
Sa tête est minuscule, barbue filiforme

sa tête est grosse comme un oignon
dans les bras d'une mère
où va-t-elle porter cet oignon:
sa poitrine est si grande!
sur la route au-dessus du toit des maisons:

pourquoi cet oignon passe-t-il tout droit?

Theatre of the Confluence (A Carixa)

A little river and a big river
the story of the bronchials
Some of the earth's heartbeat but not all

The water rose in the little river
and washed the big river away
Some of the lungs' telluric memory

The story of a river mouth
and a confluence
From such a place you can hear the river
or you can breathe
but you have to choose or it chooses you

If it chooses you you are an asthmatic
Now you can live here forever
You can sit under the oak leaves and feel wet spray

The big river and the little river
The story of a breath in a meander

The big river and the little river
A little story of leaves the river swept away

Théâtre de la confluence (a Carixa)

Une petite rivière et une grande rivière
une histoire de voies respiratoires
Un peu de battements du coeur de la terre mais pas tous

L'eau a monté dans la petite rivière
et elle a emporté la grande rivière au loin
Une partie de la mémoire tellurique des poumons

L'histoire de la bouche d'un fleuve
et d'une confluence
D'un tel endroit tu peux entendre la rivière
ou tu peux respirer
mais tu dois choisir sinon ça te prend

Si ça te prend tu es une asthmatique
Maintenant tu peux vivre ici à jamais
Tu peux t'asseoir sous les feuilles du chêne et sentir la bruine

La grande rivière et la petite rivière
Méandres de l'histoire du souffle

La grande rivière et la petite rivière
Une petite histoire de feuilles que la rivière a emportées

BARRY CALLAGHAN
TRANSLATES ANDREI VOZNESENSKY (Russian)

I began translating Andrei Voznesensky's poetry in 1967. He was one of the three most talented Soviet poets of the time. Yevtushenko, the least talented, was the best known. He seemed to operate with a certain ease and aplomb under the Soviets. Brodsky, the most talented, was also the one most at odds with the Soviet regime, and he ended up in the United States. In between was Voznesensky, an uneven poet who had produced a large body of work in various styles – moving from simple lyrics and narrative verse to hybrid experiments; a combination of poetry and prose. So, too, his subjects were varied; he had written love songs, poems of philosophical comment, satires and parodies, and poems of a certain social/historical outrage (dangerous in the Soviet Union).

The first poem I translated was a war poem, "Goya." I should say a word about the difficulties of translating from Russian into English. Russian tends to be trochaic or dactylic and English is iambic (try listening to the original soundtrack of Eisenstein's *Ivan the Terrible*, and then listen to any number of great actors playing Shakespeare and you will hear the point, and also you will hear the lugubrious sorrowful menace or menace of sorrow that seems built into Russian, indeed, to my ear, into all the Slavic languages; it is a music in the minor key). Then, Voznesensky's verbal texture is tricky; he plays with the sound of verbal roots and uses much alliteration. Finally, he uses a rhyme system that defies imitation in English, so it is best left alone. From my point of view, once you have accepted the fact that a translation can never give all the resonances and layerings of the original – and why should you expect it to do so? – one could do worse than accept Robert Lowell's idea that translation requires not just a new rendering, but a new poetry. This, of course, leads to a kind a madness... what I call Chinese water pleasure... the slow drip drip drip of single words in the brain... a drip that goes on for years.

So it has been for me with "Goya." I published my first version in 1967. In Russian, the first line has power: – *Ya Goy-ya.* Yes, yes... But – *I am Goya!* How limp. How inadequate. And it sets the tone for the whole poem. And to top it off, I could not stand – *O grapes of wrath, with a volley I hurled...* etc.

I came up with new versions in 1970 and 1973. Then I printed a "final" version in 1974. In that version I solved one problem. Walking down the street, out of nowhere I heard Melville's great cry but before I uttered the name Ismael I said Goya... and that was it; I was exultant – *Call me Goya.* It worked. Success, after seven years. Then in 1984, I solved – again to my ear – that *O grapes of wrath* line, and I published the poem again in 2005. But a reader questioned lines 6 and 7, and the reader was right; so now – having been given the opportunity again – I have come up with a new and I think satisfactory rendering of lines 6 and 7. So here it is... "Goya"... finished. Haw! Drip drip drip.

As for the hybrid poem, "The Ditch," I met Voznesensky around 1985 in Toronto, at my house. We talked about Moscow and Leningrad and we got along. To my surprise and pleasure, Voznesensky whipped a manuscript out of his pocket and said, "Why not translate this?" Which I did. But by the time I had done so, the Berlin Wall had come down and everything had changed and I never did get in touch with Voznesensky again. I published my first version in *Exile: A Literary Quarterly*, and now publish a rearranged selection from "The Ditch" here.

Гойя

Я – Гойя
Глазницы воронок мне выклевал ворог,
слетая на поле нагое.

Я – Горе.

Я – голос войны, городов головни
на снегу сорок первого года.

Я – голод.

Я – горло
повешенной бабы, чье тело, как колокол,
било над площадью голой...

Я – Гойя!

О, грозди
возмездья! Взвил залпом на Запад –
я пепел незваного гостя!

И в мемориальное небо вбил крепкие
звезды – как гвозди.

Я – Гойя.

Goya

Call me Goya!
Shock troops made shell-holes
of my eyes, a stricken field.

Call me grief.

Call me the ember of burned out towns
buried in the snows of '41.

Call me hunger.

Call me the gullet
of a garotted woman's body tolling
above the bald square.

Call me Goya!

Grapes
of wrath, enemy ashes strewn through the indelible
sky, stars ringing like hammered nails, O...

Call me Goya.

Ров

7 апреля 1986 года мы с приятелями ехали от Симферополя по Феодосийскому шоссе. Часы на щитке таксиста показывали 10 утра. Сам таксист Василий Федорович Лесных, лет эдак шестидесяти, обветренно румяный, грузный, с синими, выцветшими от виденного глазами, вновь и вновь повторял свою тягостную повесть. Здесь, под городом, на 10-м километре, во время войны было расстреляно 12 тысяч мирных жителей, главным образом еврейской национальности.

«Ну мы, пацаны, мне десять лет тогда было, бегали смотреть, как расстреливали. Привозили их в крытых машинах. Раздевали до исподнего. От шоссе шел противотанковый ров. Так вот, надо рвом их и били из пулемета. Кричали они все страшно – над степью стон стоял. Был декабрь. Все снимали галоши. Несколько тыщ галош лежало. Мимо по шоссе ехали телеги. Солдаты их не стеснялись. Солдаты все пьяные были. Заметив нас, дали по нас очередь. Да, еще вспомнил – столик стоял, где паспорта отбирали. Вся степь была усеяна паспортами. Многих закапывали полуживыми. Земля дышала.

Потом мы в степи нашли коробочку из-под гуталина. Тяжелая. В ней золотая цепочка была и две монеты. Значит, все сбережения семьи. Люди с собой несли самое ценное. Потом я слышал, кто-то вскрывал это захоронение, золотишко откапывал. Два года назад их судили. Ну об этом уже вы в курсе...»

«...У меня сосед есть, Валя Переходник. Он, может, один из всех и спасся. Его мать по пути из машины вытолкнула».

Вылезаем. Василий Федорович заметно волнуется.

The Ditch

A Spiritual Proceeding

On April 7, the year 1986, I went with some friends from Simferopol along the Feodosisky highway. Ten in the morning on the taxi driver's dashboard clock. The driver, Vasilly Fedorovich Lesnikh[1], nearly sixty years old, with faded blue eyes (he'd seen too much), told and retold his painful tale. Here, about 10 kilometers outside the city, some twelve thousand peaceful citizens were shot during the war, predominantly of Jewish nationality.

"So me and the boys, I was ten then, took off to watch the shooting. They drove them up in covered trucks. Stripped to their underwear. An anti-tank ditch angled off the highway. So, they machine-gunned them standing over the ditch. They all screamed like mad—a groan settled over the steppe. It was December. They all took off their galoshes. Thousands of galoshes lying there. Wagons went by on the highway. None of the soldiers were ashamed. The soldiers were dead drunk. Seeing us, they squeezed off a round. Sure, it's all still clear—a small table stood where they took their passports from them. The whole steppe was littered with passports. They buried a lot of people half-alive. The earth breathed.

"Then, we found a little boot-black box on the steppe. Heavy. A gold chain and two coins in it. In other words, a family's life savings. People took their valuables with them. I heard later that someone opened the burial ground, they were digging up the gold. Next year they were put on trial. But you know all that already..."

"...I have a neighbour, Vasilly Perekhodnik[2]. It could be he's the only one who was actually saved. His mother shoved him off the moving truck."

We get out. Vasilly Fedorovich is visibly upset.

---

[1] The name Lesnikh means "Forest".
[2] The name Perekhodnik means "One who crosses a boundary".

И вдруг – что это?! На пути среди зеленого поля чернеет квадрат свежевырытого колодца; земля сыра еще. За ним – другой. Вокруг груды закопченных костей, истлевшая одежда. Черные, как задымленные, черепа. «Опять роют, сволочи!» - Василий Федорович осел весь.

Сморщенный женский сапожок. Боже мой, волосы, скальп, детские рыжие волосы с заплетенной косичкой! Как их туго заплетали, верно, на что-то еще надеясь, утром перед расстрелом...

Какие сволочи! Это не литературный прием, не вымышленные герои, не страницы уголовной хроники, это мы, рядом с несущимся шоссе, стоим перед грудой человеческих черепов. Это не злодеи древности сделали, а наши, наши люди. Кошмар какой-то!

Черепа лежали грудой, эти загадки мирозданья – коричнево-темные от долгих подземных лет, - словно огромные грибы-дымовики.

Глубина профессионально вырытых шахт – около двух человеческих ростов, у одной внизу отходит штрек. На дне второй лежит припрятанная, присыпанная совковая лопата – значит сегодня придут докапывать?!

Ты куда ведешь, ров?

⁂

Рядом – черный,
как гриб-дымовик, закопчен.
Он усмешку собрал в кулачок.

⁂

ДЕЛО

Ты куда ведешь, ров?

Убивали их в декабре 1941 года. Симферопольская акция – одна из запланированных и проведенных рейхом. Ты куда ведешь, ров, куда?

And suddenly—what do we see? On the path, there in the green fields, a black square, a freshly dug pit; the earth still damp. Beyond it, another. Heaps of soot-covered bones all around and rotted clothing. Skulls so black they seemed covered in soot. "The scum are digging again." Vasilly Fedorovich said it all.

A woman's wrinkled boot. My God, hair, a scalp, a child's braided red hair. Tightly braided, with care, still hoping for something after the shooting:—the morning.

What scum! This is no literary device, no fictional hero, no page from a criminal chronicle; it's us, beside a high-speed highway, standing in front of a stack of human skulls. These aren't criminals who have done this, but our own people, today. A nightmare!

Skulls lay in a heap, riddles of the universe—a burnt sienna after long years underground—enormous smoked mushrooms. The skilfully dug pits were about the depth of two men. A tunnel had been dug at the bottom of one pit. On the second day, another hidden spade lay there—did that mean they'd be back today to finish digging?

Where are you taking me, ditch?

*

Close by—a black skull,
a smoked mushroom, smoored in soot.
A grin gathers into a fist.

*

The Case

Where are you taking me, ditch?

They killed them in December 1941. The Simferopol Action— the kind the Reich planned and carried out. Where are you off to, ditch, where?

В дело № 1586.

«…систематически похищали ювелирные изделия из захоронения на 10-м километре. В ночь на 21 июня 1984 года, пренебрегая нормами морали, из указанной могилы похитили золотой корпус карманных часов весом 35,02 г из расчета 27 рублей 30 коп. за гр, золотой браслет 30 г стоимостью 810 руб. – всего на 3325 руб. 68 коп. … 13 июля похитили золотые коронки и мосты общей стоимостью 21 925 руб., золотое кольцо 900-й пробы с бриллиантом стоимостью 314 руб. 14 коп. , четыре цепочки на сумму 1360 руб., золотой дукат иностранной чеканки стоимостью 609 руб. 65 коп., 89 монет царской чеканки стоимостью 400 руб. каждая… (т. 2 л. д. 65 – 70)».

Кто был в деле? Врач московского института АН, водитель «Межколхозстроя», рабочие, крановщик, два члена партии, местная шишка, прикативший на собственной «Волге», привезенной из загранкомандировки. Возраст 28 – 50 лет. Отвечали суду, поблескивая золотым коронками. Двое имели полный рот «красного золота». Сроки они получили небольшие, пострадали больше те, кто перепродавал. Подтверждено, что получили они как минимум 68 тысяч рублей дохода. Одного спросили: « Как Вы себя чувствовали, роя?» Ответил: «А что бы вы чувствовали, вынимая золотой мост, поврежденный пулей? Или вытащив детский ботиночек с остатком кости?»

✳

Черепа. Тамерлан. Не вскрывайте гробниц!
Разразится оттуда война.
Не порежьте лопатой
духовных грибниц!
Повылазит страшней, чем чума.

To Case No. 1586.

"... systematically purloined articles of jewellery from the
burial place at the 10th kilometer. On the night of June 21,
1984, disregarding moral norms, they did purloin from the
aforesaid grave a gold pocket watch case weighing 35.02 grams
calculated at 27 rubles 30 kopecks per gram, a gold bracelet
of 30 grams worth 810 rubles—the whole valued at 3325 rubles
68 kopecks... on June 13 they stole gold crowns and bridges,
to a total value of 21,925 rubles, a gold ring of 900 carats with
a diamond worth 314 rubles 14 kopecks, four chains to the
sum of 1360 rubles, a gold ducat of foreign coinage worth
609 rub. 65 kop., 89 coins of the Tsar's coinage worth 400 rub.
each (vol. 2, pages 65-70)."

Who stood trial? An institute doctor from Moscow—the
Academy of Sciences—an "Interkolhoz" driver, a worker, an
auxiliary worker, a movie theatre attendant. Russians, an
Azerbaijanian, a Ukrainian, an Armenian. Ages 28-50. They
confronted the court, gold crowns gleaming. Two with mouths
full of "red gold". They got short sentences—the fences were
hit harder. It checked out that they made a minimum of
68,000 rubles. One was asked: "What's it feel like, digging?"
He replied: "How would you feel, yanking out a gold bridge
broken by a bullet? Or swiping a kid's little boot with a bit
of a bone in it?"

⁂

Skulls. Tamerlane. Lock up the tombs!
War will break out.
Don't split spiritual
Mushroom spawn with a spade!
Something worse than plague will slither out.

Копали при свете фар. С летнего неба, срываясь, падали зарницы, будто искры иных лопат, работающих за горизонтом. Ты куда ведешь, ров?

They dug by the light of high beams. Lightning fell out of the summer sky, like sparks on the earth from other shovels, working the horizon. Where are you taking me, ditch?

GEORGE ELLIOTT CLARKE

TRANSLATES ALEXANDER PUSHKIN (Russian)

On Not (Really) Translating Pushkin

As an Africadian – or African Nova Scotian – I grew up in apartheid-like Halifax, Nova Scotia, in the 1960s and 1970s, glad to discover positive images of people who looked like me and mine. As a child, I knew of a host of African-American heroes, from slave emancipator Harriet Tubman to peanut butter inventor George Washington Carver, and from Civil Rights Movement radical Malcolm X, to soul singer James Brown. I also knew of the great African-Canadian contralto Portia White (1913-1968) because she was my great-aunt. When I began to write poetry, at the age of 15, I began to learn about "Blacks"– or folks of (partial) African/Negro heritage – who had won praise as European writers, namely, Alexandre Dumas, Elizabeth Barrett Browning, Colette, and, chief among them, Alexander Pushkin. As a "visible minority" poet in a coldly racialist Canada, a land of openly white supremacist imagery and politics, the example of Pushkin – a proud "Negro" and a proud Russian, beloved by all Russians – has permitted me to fantasize occasionally that maybe Africadian I could write well enough to win a smidgen of my Canadian compatriots' regard. Hence, I have given Pushkin's surname to a character in my narrative verse, and among three of my poems translated into Finnish in 2007, there is one dedicated to Pushkin (whose museum I visited in Saint Petersburg, Russia, in 2007). For me, then, Pushkin is an easy choice for a poet I would "translate."

However, I am no translator and I know no Russian. Thus, my approach has been parasitic in the extreme: I have chosen three brief poems, translated from Russian into English by scholars who knew what they were doing, and have rewritten them according to my own diction and imagery. If the original translations were already (likely) "unfaithful" approximations of the Russian models, my rewrites are even more radically separate. The one good and scary thing to be said about my renderings is, there can be no confusion between Pushkin's "makings" and my knock-offs.

Поэту

Поэт! Не дорожи любовию народной.
Восторженных похвал пройдет минутный шум;
Услышишь суд глупца и смех толпы холодной,
Но ты останься тверд, спокоен и угрюм.

Ты царь: живи один. Дорогою свободной
Иди, куда влечет тебя свободный ум,
Усовершенствуя плоды любимых дум,
Не требуя наград за подвиг благородный.

Они в самом тебе. Ты сам свой высший суд;
Всех строже оценить умеешь ты свой труд.
Ты им доволен ли, взыскательный художник?

Доволен? Так пускай толпа его бранит
И плюет на алтарь, где твой огонь горит,
И в детской резвости колеблет твой треножник.

To the Poet

(After the translation by Constance Garnett)

Poet! Damn you if you crave public love!
People clap raucously, then, fickle, stop.
Fools don scholars' mortars, bray their critiques,
While crowds' guffaws must chill your soul's marrow.
Best to stand Caesar-calm, statue-austere:
It is majesty to dwell distantly,
Palaced in your own soul, free and aloof.
Perfect your flowers, distill their liqueur-dreams,
Ignoring all praise of your past confections.
Judge for yourself the success of your art:
Your own strict taste dictates your flowers' sweetness.
Do you want joy? Let the pack bay and howl;
Let them snarl and spit on your altar's flames
And breathe your temple's triumphant perfumes.

Я вас любил

Я вас любил: любовь еще, быть может,
В душе моей угасла не совсем;
Но пусть она вас больше не тревожит;
Я не хочу печалить вас ничем.

Я вас любил безмолвно, безнадежно,
То робостью, то ревностью томим;
Я вас любил так искренно, так нежно,
Как дай вам бог любимой быть другим.

I Loved You Once

(After the translation by Dudley Randall)

I loved you once; hence tranquility quails,
For love still trembles all my flesh and frame.
But, darling, let no cross wind trouble your sails,
For though I'm hurt, love, I bear you no blame.

I loved you recklessly, in pure surrender,
Welcomed sorrows, jealousies, black and blue.
A love as intense and intent and tender,
God let another lover tender you.

Старик

Уж я не тот любовник страстный,
Кому дивился прежде свет:
Моя весна и лето красно
Навек прошли, пропал и след.
Амур, бог возраста младого!
Я твой служитель верный был;
Ах, если б мог родиться снова,
Уж так ли б я тебе служил!

Old Man (After Marot)

(After the translation by Babette Deutsch)

Lost now my nights of playboy riot,
When hot wooing set gals ablaze.
Now, April's dead, August's quiet,
And pains cool once-hot-blooded days.

Sweet Eros, youth's idol, I gave you
Everything, and God knows it's fact.
I'd serve you now—if I could have you—
Priapic faculties intact.

GEOFFREY COOK
TRANSLATES *RAINER MARIA RILKE* (German)

I studied German at university so I could read Rilke, having fallen in love with his myth of the poet and of the redemptive role of art – to "en-soul" the world and manifest the earth's consciousness. Years of reading, and reading about Rilke, and my various attempts to translate his poems, have sobered youthful romanticism, yet I think Rilke's work can still teach us the art of poetry, particularly his *New Poems* where he set about so deliberately making poems about things he saw. Derived from Rodin's lessons in seeing and working, Rilke's notion of Ding-Gedicht (thing-poem) is comparable to Eliot's more familiar and contemporary "objective co-relative". "Opium Poppy" thematizes the idea of Ding-Gedicht and, with its particularly bizarre imagery and one tumbling sentence, exemplifies what Rilke's poetics entailed and so excited me: his piling up of metaphor and the dynamics of his syntax, so integral to meaning.

The ideal conception of poetic translation – reproducing in one language that which has been created in another, including imagery, syntax, metre, rhyme, and tone – is like assuming you can "see" the "Black Cat": in fact, that possessive gaze only reflects yourself, looking. So I chose to translate poems wherein I caught glimpses of myself or of my world, hoping that this tension between recreating Rilke's vision and refracting my own would result in an authentic poetic experience. Whatever inevitably had to change from one language to another had to be meaningful in reference to the integrity of the poem and the event of translation. I was happiest with what I got away with in rhyme and rhythm and advantaged because contemporary English poetry, having purged its own anxieties, has made elbow room in looser lines and rhymes, evidenced in "Black Cat" particularly. I at least exploited organic tensions, as in "Lunatics in the Garden" where the threat of comic effect (so inappropriate for this most un-ironic of poets) from the English triplet I use in the second stanza is subdued by the somber image of the madmen futilely "circling" like Dante's sinners.

Changes of imagery in translating are more suspect today since modernism, discrediting rhyme and rhythm, over-determined the image. In what I found to be the most difficult of Rilke's poems to translate, "Opium Poppy", I've altered or added images to help visualize the poem and bring the tone home, so to speak. Rilke's "Kothurne" refers to what we might call "platform shoes" worn by actors in ancient Greek tragedies, so they could be better seen by the spectators. It is the specific image of thick-soled shoes rather than the allusion to Greek tragedy that is important, so I use "theatrical stilts", adding the term "mummers" for a more local colour. Besides, theatricality certainly animates the poem. And "Abseits im Garten...", literally "behind the garden", I translate as, "Out back the garden...", a rural Eastern Canadian colloquialism.

Like the French "étranger", the German adjective "fremd" can mean either "strange" or "foreign"; English forces the choice. Rilke's "Fremde Familie" is a disturbing poem, where I was forced to make choices if not forcing choices. The poem's anxiety concerning others and otherness is one of the thematic dualities generated by the poetics of New Poems and its intensely self-conscious dialectic of subject and object. But to merely fear the foreign or be seduced by the strange have proven moral cul-de-sacs in our century; we must, instead, through translation, be enriched by the strangeness of the foreign.

Irre im Garten Dijon

Noch schießt die aufgegebene Kartause
sich um den Hof, als würde etwas heil.
Auch die sie jetzt bewohnen, haben Pause
und nehmen nicht am Leben draußen teil.

Was irgend kommen konnte, das verlief.
Nun gehn sie gerne mit bekannten Wegen,
und trennen sich und kommen sich entgegen,
als ob sie kreisten, willig, primitiv.

Zwar manche pflegen dort die Frühlingsbeete,
demütig, dürftig, hingekniet;
aber sie haben, wenn es keiner sieht,
eine verheimlichte, verdrehte

Gebärde für das zarte frühe Gras,
ein prüfendes, verschüchtertes Liebkosen:
denn das ist freundlich, und das Rot der Rosen
wird vielleicht drohend sein und Übermaß

und wird vielleicht schon wieder übersteigen,
was ihre Seele wiederkennt und weiß.
Dies aber läßt sich noch verschweigen:
wie gut das Gras ist und wie leis.

Lunatics in the Garden

The abandoned monastery still wraps around
the courtyard, as if something'd heal.
Those living there take a break as well
and no part in the life outside.

Whatever could have happened's passed.
They walk happily now on familiar paths,
coming upon each other and going past,
as though they circled, willing, primitive.

Some there tending to the flower beds—
humble, shabby, and on their knees—
still have, when no one sees,
a surreptitious and distorted

gesture for the soft, new grass,
an intimidated, tentative caress:
for it is friendly, while the red of the rose
may frighten them in its excess

and wholly overwhelm what their souls
have recognized and understood.
This, at least, they keep secret though:
how young the grass is and how good.

Die Irren

Und sie schweigen, weil die Scheidewände
weggenommen sind aus ihrem Sinn,
und die Stunden, da man sie verstände,
heben an und gehen hin.

Nächtens oft, wenn sie ans Fenster treten:
plötzlich ist es alles gut.
Ihre Hände liegen im Konkreten,
und das Herz ist hoch und könnte beten,
und die Augen schauen ausgeruht

auf den unverhofften, oftentstellten
Garten im beruhigten Geviert,
der im Widerschein der fremden Welten
weiterwächst und niemals sich verliert.

The Lunatics

And they keep quiet because the room
dividers in their minds have been removed;
and the hours when you would understand them
have been hoisted up and hauled away.

At night when they step up to the windows
everything is suddenly okay.
Their hands lie on the tangible;
they can pray, their hearts being full,
and their eyes can calmly gaze

on the unexpected, usually distorted
garden in its now tranquil square,
which, reflecting foreign worlds,
keeps widening without ever getting lost.

Fremde Familie

So wie der Staub, der irgendwie beginnt
und nirgends ist, zu unerklärtem Zwecke
an einem leeren Morgen in der Ecke
in die man sieht, ganz rasch zu Grau gerinnt,

so bildeten sie sich, wer weiß aus was,
im letzten Augenblick vor deinen Schritten
und waren etwas Ungewisses mitten
im nassen Niederschlag der Gasse, das

nach dir verlangte. Oder nicht nach dir.
Denn eine Stimme, wie vom vorigen Jahr,
sang dich zwar an und blieb doch ein Geweine;
und eine Hand, die wie geliehen war,
kam zwar hervor und nahm doch nicht die deine.
Wer kommt denn noch? Wen meinen diese vier?

Foreign Family

Just as dust—which starts somehow
and is nowhere—for some obscure
reason on an empty morning in the corner
of blank stares, quickly clots to grey,

so they took shape—from who knows what—
in the second before your footsteps,
and were something dubious amidst
the damp trash of the alley that

longed for you. Or not.
For a voice as from last year
did sing to you, yet was still like weeping;
and a hand, which seemed to be reaching
out, was extended and yet did not take yours.
What's next? Who do they think they are?

Schwarze Katze

Ein Gespenst ist noch wie eine Stelle,
dran dein Blick mit einem Klange stößt;
aber da, an diesem schwarzen Felle
wird dein stärkstes Schauen aufgelöst:

wie ein Tobender, wenn er in vollster
Raserei ins Schwarze stampft,
jählings am benehmenden Gepolster
einer Zelle aufhört und verdampft.

Alle Blicke, die sie jemals trafen,
scheint sie also an sich zu verhehlen,
um darüber drohend und verdrossen
zuzuschauern und damit zu schlafen.
Doch auf einmal kehrt sie, wie geweckt,
ihr Gesicht und mitten in das deine:
und da triffst du deinen Blick im geelen
Amber ihrer runden Augensteine
unerwartet wieder: eingeschlossen
wie ein ausgestorbenes Insekt.

Black Cat

Even a ghost is like a place your glance
clangs up against;
but in that black pelt
your hardest stare disintegrates:

just as a lunatic in the full tide of his rage
stomps off into the dark
only to stop short at the patient
padding of a cell and evaporate.

All the looks that ever lay upon her
she seems to hide within herself
so she can mull them over,
morose and menacing, then nap with them.

But all at once, as if awakened,
she turns her face straight
into your own, where you recognize
what you least expect
embedded in the amber of her stony eyes:
your own gaze, like some extinct insect.

Schlaf-Mohn

Abseits im Garten blüht der böse Schlaf,
in welchem die, die heimlich eingedrungen,
die Liebe fanden junger Spiegelungen,
die willig waren, offen und konkav,

und Träume, die mit aufgeregten Masken
auftraten, riesiger durch die Kothurne—:
das alles stockt in diesen oben flasken
weichlichen Stengeln, die die Samenurne

(nachdem sie lang, die Knospe abwärts tragend,
zu welken meinten) festverschlossen heben:
gefranste Kelche auseinanderschlagend,
die fieberhaft das Mohngefäß umgeben.

Opium Poppy

Out back the garden blooms that evil sleep,
where those who secretly broke in
discovered the love of young reflections—
all concave, willing, open—
and dreams that stepped up like mummers in freaked-out masks,
even more immense on theatrical stilts:

all this festers in the topmost flasks
of the feeble stems, which (their buds drooping,
having long intended to wilt)
raise the tightly closed seed urn,
round which, flailing asunder, the frayed calyx
feverishly chokes the poppy-chalice.

CHRISTOPHER DODA

TRANSLATES *LEOPOLD STAFF* (Polish)

(with assistance in the Polish by Peter Figura)

Though Polish poet Leopold Staff (1878-1957) is virtually unknown to the English language, his presence is felt through the works of oft-translated poets whom he influenced: Miłosz, Szymborska, Herbert and, especially, Różewicz. Between 1901 and 1954, he produced 16 collections of poetry (a 17th was released posthumously), numerous plays and a great deal of translations from Latin, French, Italian and German. As a figure whose career spanned the neo-Romantic and Symbolist concerns of the late-19th century to the Modernist mid-20th century and who produced his greatest works in his old age, his closest canonical counterpart for us would be Yeats. And yet, this incredibly prolific poet has only been translated once in book form in English: a slender volume called *An Empty Room* (ed. Adam Czerniawski) in 1983. I chose Staff almost entirely based on this neglect.

Translating Staff was a multi-step process. I first took his five-volume, 1100 page collected verse out of the library and pored over it using my grandmother's 1926 Polish-English dictionary. Once I narrowed the selection down to 13 pieces (they are drawn from the 1930s with the exceptions of "Mythology" and "Saint Sebastian," both published in 1946), I sought the assistance of a Polish speaker in Toronto, to provide literal translations of the poems and to read them aloud to me so I could get a 'feel' for the language. I quickly surmised that preserving the cadence of Polish into English would be impossible, as they sound nothing alike, so I opted to replicate it with a cadence associated with English verse. It was thus my job to take the literal translations and render them into poetry, and to preserve the rhyme and meter that are intrinsic to Staff's style. In the end, I finished ten and used the six that best preserved the spirit of the original.

With my thanks to Peter Figura for his invaluable assistance in preparing these translations.

Ars Poetica

Echo z dna serca, nieuchwytne,
Woła mi: «Schwyć mnie, nim przepadnę,
Nim zblednę, stanę się błękitne,
Srebrzyste, przezroczyste, żadne!»

Łowię je spiesznie jak motyla,
Nie abym świat dziwnością zdumiał,
Lecz by się kształtem stała chwila
I abyś, bracie, mnie zrozumiał.

I niech wiersz, co ze strun się toczy,
Będzie, przybrawszy rytm i dźwięki,
Tak jasny jak spojrzenie w oczy
I prosty jak podanie ręki.

Ars Poetica

A poem is an echo of a thought
That says "Catch me before I disappear,
Before I fade, before I'm wrought
Solid or transparent or neither."

So I net it like a butterfly,
Write it down, not to astound
But to forge a moment as reality
And for you, my brother, to understand.

Let the poem be like music, it relies
Upon rhythm and sound to make
It as clear as a look in the eyes,
As simple as a handshake.

Pojednanie

Gdy idę w zachód, o słonecznym skłonie,
W świetle i ogniu kopuły niebieskiej,
Stąpają przy mnie, dzierżąc mnie za dłonie,
Anioł żebraczy i szatan królewski.

Wieczyście wrodzy sobie, jak bieguny,
We mnie się z sobą stapiają w przymierze
I spływa na mnie, w zmierzchu złotej łuny,
Pewność spokojna jak kroczenie w wierze.

I już o żadnym niebie nie pamięta
Ani się piekłem żadnym nie udręcza
Dusza, radością i bólem rozpięta
Na cichym niebie, jak krzyż i jak tęcza.

Reconciliation

As I walk toward sunset, I hear
Two voices: one good, one evil.
They hold my hands, the angel of a beggar
And for the king, a devil.

Eternal enemies achieve détente
In my being, their union must
Glow in the twilight; a fount
Born of quiet trust

That recalls no Paradise
Nor burns like Inferno,
Is splayed against the skies
Like the cross and the rainbow.

Wróg

Hipnotyzer oszalał,
Że mnie uśpić nie może.
Oczy wściekłą krwią zalał
I wbił we mnie jak noże.

Ślepia swe w mózg mi wtrzeszcza
Wolę swą w rdzeń mój wsila.
Gnie mnie przemoc złowieszcza,
Ulegnę lada chwila.

Od wzrocznego zastrzyku
Pierś mą chwyta zadyszka.
Przewierca mnie do szpiku
Spojrzenie bazyliszka.

Sięga mych sił granicy,
Lecz mój opór przemaga.
Przemy się zapaśnicy,
Waha się równowaga.

Wreszcie płomiennooki
Do cna moc swą osłabił
I wpadł w sen tak głęboki,
Że na miejscu się zabił.

An Enemy

The hypnotist went nuts
Trying to put me under.
He hated my guts—
He's so severe.

His will is great
At the flanks of my soul
And he lives to berate
The most precious goal

I can confess:
I am where my mind lies.
But he sees only 'yes'
Through basilisk eyes.

So he pushes my limits,
Tests my defence
As our tumbling, wrestling gimmicks
Push us into balance

Until my gaze is deep,
Until he's in despair,
Until he falls asleep,
Dies right then and there.

Droga

Skacz w ciemną topiel, niech najszerzej kryśli
    Swych kręgów słoje.
Rzucaj się w myśli wielkie: wielkie myśli
    To niepokoje.

Przez nie jedynie samotna i stroma
    Prowadzi droga,
Choć nienazwana, chociaż niewiadoma,
    Do swego Boga.

Ale się dusza nie utrzyma na dnie
    Czy u zenitu.
Wypłynie z nurtem na wierzch albo spadnie
    Z połowy szczytu.

Nigdy nie dotrze, chociaż się przybliży,
    Chociaż przeczuje.
Gdzie szukam, zawsze jest głębiej i wyżej,
    Niż gdzie znajduję.

The Way

Plunge into the deep pool and let its circles
    Spread far out.
Plunge into brilliant ideas; great miracles
    Shall sprout

On the lonely, steep and nameless path
    That winds
Past the edge of the sacred bath
    To the divine.

My soul will not stay below the water
    Near the river's edge.
It will emerge from under, or falter
    At the ledge.

Always elusive, the peace that I search
    For, true calm
Is deeper and farther, just out of reach
    From wherever I am.

Mitologia

Nie pamiętam gór. Dawno ich już nie widziałem.
Pewnie znikły i pono wyschły wielkie morza.
W niskich bagnach odbija się zachodnia zorza
I oświeca mrok klęski, co stała się ciałem.

Konają pola, rodzą się tylko cmentarze,
Pioruny zamieniły w gruz świątynie miasta,
Modlitwy szept w przekleństwo rozpaczy urasta,
A w kostnicy pijani śmieją się grabarze.

Zdejmcie wędzidła świętym rumakom. Powrozem
Spętane, nie pogonią—skubiąc trawę w rowie.
Wyłupiono bogini mądre oczy sowie
I ogień na ołtarzu zgaszono nawozem.

Na drodze ciemne błoto. W niebie szara chmura.
A gościńcem, skazany na żywot tułaczki,
Idzie kulawy anioł, wlokąc ciężkie taczki,
W których leżą wydarte z jego skrzydeł pióra.

Mythology

The mountains are gone a long time now. Perhaps forever.
They were ground down with the drying of the seas
In broken earth, remnants of our lost paradise
Where over fetid swamps, dawn spread over

Fields with no yield. But cemeteries flourish.
Daylight reveals the ruined temple, prayers
Once whispered become profane, words of despair.
And gravediggers drink and O how they laugh.

The crumbled icons have lost their jewelled eyes
And we are just us now, normal, full of aimless discontent,
Pleased with ourselves on the surface. We meant
To forget the myth and toil away for things to buy.

But on the road, dark mud. In the sky, endless cloud.
And outside the town gates, reduced to a mendicant,
A limping angel wanders alone, drags a beggar's cart
Where all the feathers ripped from his wings reside.

Święty Sebastian

Odarty z pozłocistej zbroi pretoriańskiej,
Przytroczony do drzewa i przez pełnych buty
Zbirów na smukłym ciele strzałami pokłuty,
W nienagannej piękności, jak posąg pogański,

Kona święty Sebastian, nagi rycerz Pański,
I w górę wzrok unosi mgłą śmierci zasnuty,
W niezachwianej stałości trwać gotów dopóty,
Aż się rozpłynie duszą w światłości niebiańskiej.

I gdy, omdlały, członki łabędzimi zwisa
W powrozach, wycieńczony męczeńskimi rany,
Bielejąc od upływu świętej krwi bez ceny,

Marzy sennie o losie boskiego Odysa,
Co na morzu do masztu, jak on, przywiązany,
Słuchał, jak w dali cudnie śpiewają syreny.

Saint Sebastian

Stripped of his Praetorian armour
By former comrades, bound to a tree:
His body a target, its flawless beauty
Laid open, weak but utterly strong, for

Sebastian is dying, a saint soon,
One of God's naked boys, a death
Unique, his last murmur of breath
Will grace the lonely moon.

When he fainted into his past,
Hung in ropes and open like a wound,
He was weak as he bled his priceless blood

In pure white dreaming. Tied to a mast
On boiling seas, rapt like Odysseus
By sirens' song off in the distance.

RISHMA DUNLOP
TRANSLATES MARÍA ELENA CRUZ VARELA (Spanish)

My interest in the work of María Elena Cruz Varela is at once literary and political. I happened on her book *Balada de la sangre (Ballad of the Blood)* a few years ago at a secondhand bookstore. I was conducting research on women poets of resistance and witness and became fascinated by Varela's story and drawn in by her poems. María Elena Cruz Varela won Cuba's National Award for Poetry in 1989. This prize was given to her by the Union of Cuban Writers and Artists, which later expelled her from its ranks because of her anti-Castro political views in 1991. In May 1991, Varela organized a human rights organization called Criterio Alternativo, a known group of anti-Castro intellectuals. She and nine other writers wrote a letter to Fidel Castro, calling for greater openness in Cuba, direct elections, economic and democratic reforms, and the release of political prisoners. State-run newspapers attacked these writers as agents of the CIA. Following this act of dissent, on November 21, 1991, a state security brigade broke into her Havana apartment, where she lived with her husband, daughter, and son. She was dragged by her hair down several flights of stairs into the street. Cruz Varela was beaten in front of a cheering mob, which included a group of schoolchildren trucked in for the occasion. She was then forced to eat her manifesto before being arrested, thrown in jail, beaten, and starved. She was released in 1994 and went into exile in Puerto Rico. María Elena Cruz Varela was named a Prisoner of Conscience by Amnesty International.

The poems translated here are from a manuscript that survived and in Varela's poems are the many voices of the tortured, the silenced, the executed, and the forgotten. Her poems were written and preserved against censorship, humiliation, beatings, imprisonment. For me, the task of the translator has been to somehow preserve a voice that speaks out against a political system she refused as "a closed system of impossibilities, a system that recognizes submission to a crude ideology," in a way that remains faithful to Varela's distinctive voice. The poetics at work in the Spanish originals include a repetition of short declaratives, choppy one word phrases, unusual in English poetry, which I have retained as essential to the rhythm and impact of these poems. Varela writes a clandestine poetry of witness, subversive, dignified, and frequently, as in the poem "Circus," bordering on macabre and surreal. In the figure of the exhausted angel, the echoes of Rilke are found in the contemplations about beauty and terror that can barely be endured. At times, Varela speaks as a narrator of multiple voices heard in prison, for those lonely, tortured and executed; at other times, she speaks as a woman, lover, mother, and most importantly, the poet. "The poet saved me," Varela has claimed in an interview with Mairyim Cruz-Bernal, her translator for the first bilingual edition of *Ballad of the Blood*. Her voice is a broken voice that seeks revival. And indeed, her work is evidence of the survival of the imagination in times of violence and oppressive silencing.

Bajo el paso del fuego

Digan que estoy cansada, que soy buena
que he vendido en subasta mi agonía
que se gastó la sal en mis arenas
y pongo a secar la vida mía.

Digan que la humedad me tuvo muerta
que es muy triste bañarse con ceniza
que regalé las flores de mi huerta
y el último botón de mi camisa.

Y diganle también que se suicidan
objetos personales en mi cama
que destilo la luz por las heridas
y escribo este papel sobre la llama.

Under the Passage of Fire

Say that I am tired, that I am good
that I have auctioned off my agony
that there is no more salt in my sands
and that I hang my life out to dry.

Say that the humidity found me dead
that it is a great sorrow to bathe in ashes
that I gave away my garden flowers
and the last button on my shirt.

And say to him also that personal objects
are committing suicide on my bed.
That I distill light through my wounds
and I write this page over the flame.

El circo

Pasen. Señores. Pasen. No se detengan. Sigan.
Adéntrense hasta el fondo. Será una gran función.
Verán a los lagartos rasgándose la piel. Sin
inmutarse. Verán al fin qué pasa
detrás de mis telones. Pasen. Señores. Pasen.
No se detengan. Sigan. Pobrísimo payaso
reiré para ustedes. Lloraré para ustedes.
Haré saltar los goznes y solo para ustedes.
Seré la bailarina que galopa desnuda
mostrando centelleante el arco de su pubis.
La cadera redonda. Lo erecto de sus pechos
es también para ustedes. Toda esta gran fanfarria.
Toda esta algarabia. Este andamiaje tenso de cuerdas
para ustedes. Este clown festinado lo sirvo
para ustedes. Oropel. Aderezo.
Ofrendas de primera a los leones.
Pasen señores. Pasen. No se detengan. Sigan.
Verán como transmute en oro sus cristales.
Y travesty del odio dare los puntapiés con alegría.
Juro solemnemente: no sera doloroso. Pero pasen.
Por Dios. ¿Qué es un circo sin público?
Sin todos los ustedes que aplauden por piedad.
Por simpatía. Por hipnosis. Por miedo.
Pasen. Que pasen todos. La carpa ya está lista.
Y listos los remiendos. Los parches del apuro.
Pasen. Señores. Pasen.
Atentos los pulgares que apunten hacia arriba.
Verán todos sus sueños hecho añicos.
Es pura ilusión óptica. Verán cómo les robo

The Circus

Come, Señores. Come in. Don't hesitate. Come in.
Make your way to the back. This will be a grand spectacle.
You will see lizards scraping their skins. Without concern.
You will finally see what happens behind my curtains.
Come in, Señores. Come in. Don't hesitate. Come in.
Poor clown, I will laugh for you all. Cry for you.
I will make the hinges jump, and just for you.
I will be the dancer who gallops naked
showing the shimmering arc of her pubis
her round hips. Her erect breasts
are also for you. All this fanfare.
All this gibberish. All this backstage taut with ropes
for you. This festooned clown. I serve you all.
Sequins. Seasoning.
First-class offerings for the lions.
Come in, Señores. Come in.
You will see how I transform your crystals into gold.
A transvestite of hatred I will kick with joy.
I solemnly swear it won't be painful. But come in.
By God. What is the circus without its audience?
Without all of you who applaud in pity.
In sympathy. In hypnosis. In fear.
Come in. Everyone come in. The tent is ready.
And ready are the mendings. The patches of haste.
Come in, Señores. Come in.
Wait for the thumbs to turn up.
Wait for the thumbs to turn down.
You will see all your dreams broken in pieces.
It is a pure optical illusion. You will see how I steal

su pobre identidad con mi sombrero.
Cómo pagan mis liebres su tonta rebeldía.
Pasen. Señores. Pasen. No se detengan. Sigan.
Adéntrense hasta la fondo.

your identity with my hat.
How my rabbits pay for their foolish rebellion.
Come in, Señores, come in. Do not hesitate. Come. Continue.
Make your way to the back.

Cancion de amor para tiempos difíciles

Antonio, cuánto me dueles siendo hombre. –Albis Torres

Difícil escribir te quiero con locura.
Hasta la misma médula. ¿Qué será de mi cuerpo
si se pierden tus manos? ¿Qué sera de mis manos
si se pierde tu pelo? Difícil. Muy difícil
un poema de amor en estos tiempos.
Resulta que tú estás. Feroz en tu evidencia.
Resulta que yo estoy. Contrahecha. Asechante.
Y resulta que estamos. La ley de gravedad no nos perdona.
Difícil es decirte te quiero en estos tiempos.
Te quiero con urgencia.
Quiero hacer un aparte. Sin dudas. Y sin trampas.
Para decir te quiero. Así. Sencillamente.
Y que tu amor me salva del aullido nocturno
cuando loba demente la fiebre me arrebata.
No quiero que me duela la falta de ternura.
Pero amor. Qué difícil escribir que te quiero.
Así. *"Entre tanto gris. Tanta corcova junta."*
Cómo puedo aspirar la transparencia.
Retomar esta voz tan desgastada.
Esta costumbre antigua para decir te quiero.
Así. Sencillamente. Antiguamente. Digo.
Si todo es tan difícil. Si duele tanto todo.
Si un hombre. Y otro hombre. Y luego otro. Y otro.
Destrozan los espacios donde el amor se guarda.
Si no fuera difícil. Difícil y tremendo.
Si no fuera imposible olvidar esta rabia.
Mi reloj. Su tic-tac. La ruta hacia el cadalso.

Love Song for Difficult Times

Antonio, how much it hurts to be a man. –ALBIS TORRES

It's difficult to describe how I love you—with a kind of madness.
With the same marrow. What would happen to my body
if I lost your hands? What would happen to my hands
if I lost your hair? Difficult. Very difficult
to write a love poem in these times.
You exist. Ferocious in your evidence.
I exist. Counterfeit. Insistent.
And we exist. The law of gravity is unforgiving.
So difficult to tell you I love you in these times.
I love you with urgency.
I want to make a statement. Without doubt. Without traps.
To tell you I love you. Like that. With plain speech.
That your love will save me
from the nocturnal howl. Like the maddened
she-wolf, the fever will take me.
I don't want to be hurt by the lack of tenderness.
But love. How difficult to write that I love you.
Here. *Between so much grey, so many hunchbacks together.*
How can I aspire to transparency.
To revive this worn-out voice.
This ancient custom of saying I love you.
Like this. Plainly. In the ancient way. I say.
If everything is so difficult. If everything hurts so much.
If one man. And another man. And then another. And another.
Destroy the spaces where love is kept.
If it were not hard. Difficult and tremendous.
If it were not possible to forget this rage.

Mi sentencia ridícula con esta cuerda falsa.
Si no fuera difícil. Difícil y tremendo.
Plasmaría este verso con su cadencia cursi.
Si fuera así de simple escribir que te quiero.

My clock. Its tick-tock. The route to the scaffold.
My ridiculous sentence with this false cord.
If it weren't difficult. Difficult and tremendous.
I would cast off this verse with its cheap cadence.
If it were simple to write that I love you.

El ángel exterminador

Aquí está lo terrible. Lo hermoso abrumador. Lo destructivo.
El ángel que me roza. Aro de luz. Presencia del candor que nos fulmina
el arquero suspenso entre dos rayos. Soy infeliz. Mortal.
Debajo de la máscara sospecho las hondísimas traiciones de mi cuerpo.
Me inicio en lo terrible. Iluminándome.
Las otras que soy no me determinan. Puesto que
todo ángel anuncia el extermino. Me aferro a los maderos.
Los dejo lacerar mi pobre espalda. Arrástrense mis pies.
Es mi vía crucis. Un paso más. Un paso a la antesala del infierno.
Cómo dejar pasar las caricias mordaces de la lumbre.
Y cómo no adorar al cuerpo por el cuerpo. Al hombre en sí.
Al junco vibratorio. Variaciones del acto en que me elevo.
Fatalidad de acróbata. Lo bello. Lo terrible.
Lo insoportable eterno exhale sus burbujas. Que débil soplo soy.
Tan implorante. Hundiéndome en el cuerpo por el cuerpo.
Tratando de escapar. Y no hay salida.
Se vislumbran los restos de antiguos esplendores.
Quizás no haya más luz. Tal vez no habrá más fuego.
Quizás vuelva al país de las nieves perpetuas.
A mi disfraz de huérfana en invierno. Un ángel en la jarcia.
Acorde sigiloso de pobre aeda ciego.
Dispuesto a ejecutar mis inmundicias.
Patentizar mis actos. Mis terrores inéditos.
Un ángel es la fragua. Temedle a la belleza.
En ella se concentran la levedad y el peso.
Aquí está lo terrible. Lo hermoso destructor.
Y apenas sé si puedo soportarlo.

The Exterminating Angel

Here is the terrible thing. The beauty that overwhelms. That destroys.
The angel that brushes past me in a ring of light. Pure presence
that the archer holds between two rays. I am unhappy. Mortal.
Beneath the mask I suspect the deep treasons of my body.
I initiate myself into the terrible. I cast a light upon myself.
The other women that I am do not determine me. Because
every angel announces extermination. I cling to the rafters.
I let them lacerate my poor back. My feet dragging.
This is my Via Crucis. One more step. One way to the waiting room of hell.
How to allow the scathing caresses of the fire to pass.
How can I not worship the body for the body itself. Man himself.
The vibrating reed. Variations of the act in which I take flight.
Fatality of the acrobat. The beautiful. The terrible.
Unbearable eternity exhales its bubbles. My breath a weak murmur.
So imploring. Sinking into the body through the body.
Trying to escape. And there is no exit.
A glimpse of the remains of ancient splendors.
Perhaps there will be no more light. No more fire.
Maybe I will return to the country of perpetual snow.
To my guise of an orphan in winter. An angel in the rigging.
Line stolen from a poor blind bard.
Ready to carry out my filth.
To patent my acts. My unbelievable terrors.
An angel is the forge. Be afraid of beauty.
In it, lightness and weight are held.
Here is the terrible thing. The beauty that destroys.
And I barely know if I can endure it.

Se van los que yo quiero

También te marcharás, como José.
No podré conocer tu nombre verdadero.
No podré descifrar tu santo y seña.
No podré saber nunca
en qué lugar del barrio está tu casa.

Yo no pude apostar
yo sólo puedo —a veces— dejar la nave al pairo
y me sirve de poco acunar las consignas.

Voy a moldear con barro una tinaja
para los peregrinos
para los como tú, con sus seudónimos
para los como tú, con sus angustias
de segundo orden
para pensar en ti sin que claudique el polen
mientras me asumo y quemo cortezas de naranja.

De nuevo irán de paso las hordas migratorias
gorriones de mi patio
yo tuve alguna vez posada sobre el hombro
un ave blanca.

Sólo sé que era blanca, intensamente blanca
con un ojo redondo y asombrado.

The Ones I Love Are Leaving

You will leave, too, like José.
I cannot know your true name.
No chance to decipher your password.
Never to know which house is yours in the quarter.

And I couldn't bet.
I could only—sometimes—leave the ship to its course.
It does not serve me to coin slogans.

I'm going to mold clay into a pitcher
for the pilgrims
for those like you with their pseudonyms
for those like you with your second order anguish
to think about you, never pollinated
while I burn the peelings of oranges.

Once again they will fly, the hordes
of sparrows migrating in my yard.
Once I found, perched on a man
a white bird.

I know only that it was white, intensely white
with one eye round and amazed.

Versión de lejanía

No quiero hacer enmiendas las cosas
sobre todo esas cosas son y son.
Un infeliz comienzo el de esta carta
pero no es mi propósito cantarle a las consignas.
Sólo voy a decirte que buscamos
un lugar en la sala para ubicar tu rostro
y reeditamos por turno tus manías.

Tanto tiempo y te escribo.
No me voy a quejar, no te preocupes.
No voy a hacer listados de miserias domésticas
carece de sentido si estamos tan clavados
a esta humedad del trópico.

Cuando miro a los hijos
les quisiera explicar que estoy en dos mitades:
si a veces contradigo, nunca estoy antagónica
que si anuncio me agoto, la piel se me marchita
estoy hasta los pelos, al borde de la histeria
quiero decir te amo, quiero hacer el amor
pero contigo.
Entonces lloro y lloro
viro al revés las fotos
que no tienen angustias, que no nos envejecen.

Después me deposito, tiemblo y vuelvo a ver claro
te invento o te imagino en los protagonistas
de los filmes del sábado.
No me veas ridícula
con la influencia cursi del cinema barato
pero creces y creces

Version of the Far Away

I do not wish to amend things
especially these things
that simply exist.
A wretched beginning to this letter
but it's not my purpose to sing slogans.
I will tell you only that we searched
in the living room to find your face
and turn by turn we re-edited your manias.

Such a long time has passed and now I write to you.
I won't complain; don't worry.
I won't make lists of domestic miseries;
these make no sense, nailed
as we are to this tropical humidity.

When I look at the children
I want to explain that I am split in two:
if I am sometimes contradictory I'm not antagonistic.
If I announce that I am exhausted, my skin withers.
I am on the edge, at the brink of hysteria.
I want to say I love you. I want to make love
but only with you.
Then I cry and cry.
I turn the photos, live them in reverse
the ones in which we have no anxieties and
the ones that do not age us.

After, I tremble and I begin to see clearly again.
I imagine you as the star of Saturday films.
Don't think of me as ridiculous, easily influenced by corny movies
but you grow and grow

y te veo hermosísimo en traje de campaña
me revienta el orgullo, se me inflaman los pechos
es tan fuerte ese nombre: Matagalpa:
mezcla de ron con miel para aclarar las dudas.

Quiero que estés allí.
Quiero que estemos juntos.
Lavaré las paredes (por si acaso)
me haré un vestido nuevo para cuando regreses.

Cuídate, pero no demasiado
y te amaré más virgen después de este gran parto.

and I see you most beautiful in your country clothes
and I explode with pride, my breasts swell.
It's so strong that name: Matagalpa:
potion of rum and honey to clear up all doubts.

I want you there.
I want us to be together.
I'll wash the walls (just in case).
I'll make a new dress to wear for your return.

Take care of yourself, but not too much
and I will love you even more virginal after this great birth.

STEVEN HEIGHTON
TRANSLATES HORACE (Latin)

In approaching these four odes of Horace I've stuck with my usual practice as an amateur translator, giving myself the freedom to make each approximation as "free" or as "faithful" as the original inspires me to be. So "Pyrrha" sticks close to the untitled original in its structure, imagery and level of diction, while "Chloe" has morphed from an unrhymed twelve-line poem into a short-lined sonnet. "A Strange Fashion of Forsaking" is inflected and re-gendered by way of Sir Thomas Wyatt's famous poem "They Flee from Me", while "Noon on Earth!" has gone from a linguistically formal eight lines to a highly colloquial seventeen.

Robert Kroetsch once observed that every poem is a failed translation. What a translation can't afford to be is a failed poem – or at least an uninteresting one. My aim in approximating a poem that I love is, of course, to make a compelling counterpart in English – something to entertain you, startle you, pry you open – while in the process entertaining myself: sitting up, by candlelight, with dictionaries and a glass of Douro red, the house silent, even the bats in our walls asleep; reciting the original lines aloud, in some cases two thousand years after their conception; weighing how best to re-conceive those cadences in English; serving as a kind of stenographer to the dead, a medium at a prosodic séance, an avid collaborator, an apprentice always learning from the work. And for me, the most mysterious, engrossing work lies in finding a way into old or ancient poems and making them young again. Hence Horace.

I'll conclude by quoting the middle section of a poem I translated several years ago – a poem by the contemporary Italian writer Valerio Magrelli, which suggests some of the addictive bustle and exertion of the translator's work. (The unquoted opening lines introduce the metaphor of the translator as a one person moving company.)

> I too move something—words—
> to a new building, words
> not mine, setting hands to things
> I don't quite know, not quite
> comprehending what I move.
> Myself I move—translate
> pasts to presents, to presence, that
> travels sealed up, packed in pages
> or in crates . . .

The final unpacking, of course, is the task of the reader.

[The Odes] (i, 5)

Quis multa gracilis te puer in rosa
perfusus liquidis urget odoribus
   grato, Pyrrha, sub antro?
     Cui flavam religas comam,

simplex munditiis? Heu quotiens fidem
mutatosque deos flebit et aspera
   nigris aequora ventis
     emirabitur insolens

qui nunc te fruitur credulus aurea,
qui semper vacuam, semper amabilem
   sperat, nescius aurae
     fallacis. Miseri, quibus

intemptata nites. Me tabula sacer
votiva paries indicat uvida
   suspendisse potenti
     vestimenta maris deo.

Pyrrha (i, 5)

What slender elegant youth, perfumed
among roses, is urging himself on you,
  Pyrrha, in the fragrant grotto? Have you
    bound your yellow hair so gracefully

for him? How many times he'll weep because
faith is fickle, as the gods are, how often
  will the black, sea-disquieting winds
    astonish him, although for now

credulous, grasping at fool's gold, he enjoys you,
hopes you'll always be calm water, always
  this easy to love. Unconscious of the wind's wiles
    he's helpless, still tempted

by your gleaming seas. But high on the temple wall
I've set this votive tablet, and in thanks
  to the god for rescue have hung
    my sea-drenched mantle there.

[The Odes] *(i, 23)*

Vitas inuleo me similis, Chloë,
quaerenti pavidam montibus aviis
  matrem non sine vano
    aurarum et siluae metu.

Nam seu mobilibus veris inhorruit
adventus foliis, seu virides rubum
  dimovere lacertae,
    et corde et genibus tremit.

Atqui non ego te tigris ut aspera
Gaetulusve leo frangere persequor:
  tandem desine matrem
    tempestiva sequi viro.

Chloe (i, 23)

You flee from me, Chloe, a young deer
urgently in search of mother, lost
in lonely, high forests
tremulous with fear

at the mountain's slimmest breeze, or
springtime's delicate revealing
of leaves, or a leaf-green lizard's spring
from thickets. (What terrors seize

the fawn then!) But Chloe, I'm neither
a tiger nor a lion, intent
on savage appetites, or upon

causing you any pain. Forget
looking back for your mother
now, woman:
                  it's time to love a man.

[The Odes] (i, 25)

Parcius iunctas quatiunt fenestras
iactibus crebris iuvenes protervi,
nec tibi somnos adimunt, amatque
    ianua limen,

quae prius multum facilis movebat
cardines. Audis minus et minus iam:
"Me tuo longas pereunte noctes,
    Lydia, dormis?"

Invicem moechos anus arrogantis
flebis in solo levis angiportu,
Thracio bacchante magis sub inter-
    lunia vento,

cum tibi flagrans amor et libido,
quae solet matres furiare equorum,
saeviet circa iecur ulcerosum,
    non sine questu,

laeta quod pubes hedera virenti
gaudeat pulla magis atque myrto,
aridas frondes hiemis sodali
    dedicet Euro.

"A Strange Fashion of Forsaking..." (i, 25)
(via Thomas Wyatt)

The wilder girls hardly bother anymore
to rattle your shuttered window with fists or
pitch stones, shatter your dreamfree sleep, while your door,
    once oiled and swinging,

nimbly hinged, hangs dead with rust. Less and less
you wake now to ex-lovers crying, "Thomas,
you bastard, how can you sleep?—I'm dying for us
    to do it again."

Seems to me your turn's long overdue—solo
nightshift when like some codger in a cul-
de-sac you'll moan for all the women (scornful
    now) who one time sought you.

The cold will be what finds you then—northeasters
whining down in the gloom of the moon, and lust
in riddled guts twisting you like a stud in must
    who has to stand watching

his old mares mounted. You'll know then, the desire
of girls is for greener goods—such dry sticks
and wiltwood, blown only by the cold, they just figure
    who has the time for.

[The Odes] (i, 11)

Tu ne quaesieris—scire nefas—quem mihi, quem tibi
finem di dederint, Leuconoë, nec Babylonios
temptaris numeros. Ut melius quicquid erit pati,
seu pluris hiemes, seu tribuit Iuppiter ultimam,
quae nunc oppositis debilitat pumicibus mare
Tyrrhenum. Sapias, vina liques, et spatio brevi
spem longam reseces. Dum loquimur, fugerit invida
aetas: carpe diem, quam minimum credula postero.

Noon on Earth! *(starting from i, 11)*

Why trouble wondering how long
breath will last, how long your eyes
will still bask in the heavenshed
lucence of noon on earth. Horoscopes,
palmistry, the séance gild pockets
but confide nothing sure. We have to take it—
the future's shrugged *whatever,* that weather
of uncertainty—unknowing whether gods
will grant us the grey of further
winters that'll churn the sea until the sea
gnaws, noses into the littoral
of our lives, eroding whatever is
so far unclaimed.
                Enough.
Better open the red, pitch the cork, toast
our moment—tomorrow's an idle
nevering, ghost of a god
unworth such wasted faith.

Andréa Jarmai
translates George Faludy (Hungarian)

My earliest exposure to the work of Faludy came from my father quoting by heart at suitable occasions lines from Faludy's justly famous "trans-creations" – Faludy's phrase – of the ballads of François Villon.

Faludy's poems have, therefore, always been a part of my life, but it was towards the end of the millennium that I first began to translate his work into English. About that time, I also met Magdi Szenttamássy, a long-time friend of my parents, and in the course of afternoon tea it transpired that she and her husband had been good friends of Faludy through all the years he spent in Toronto.

Magdi was thrilled to hear of my translations, read them, and subsequently asked if she might send some of them to Faludy as a present for his ninetieth birthday.

Faludy wrote back to Magdi to say that the translations captured the spirit of the originals, something no previous translations of his work had done, and asked Magdi to persuade me to continue translating, as he would have them published.

Faludy himself chose my translation of "Michelangelo's Last Prayer" for the bronze plaque in George Faludy Place, the park opposite 25 St. Mary Street, where Faludy lived for most of his twenty-two years in Toronto.

From 1999, when I first began to translate his work, until his death in 2006, I considered Faludy the greatest living poet. A. E. Housman's test for good poetry – it raises the hairs on one's face as one is shaving – may be applied to Faludy's work to gratifying effect. The highest joy of translating Faludy's poetry is to try to prove equal to them in English, and, in his lifetime, to have Faludy himself deem the translations worthy. The direst challenges are the differences in structure and cadence between

Hungarian and English: to capture the spirit of the poems and still render them in rhyme and rhythm, and in the original forms; in sum, to present sonnets in the form of sonnets. In all of this I owe thanks to David Newel for his editorial help.

It is a pleasure, thus, to be able to make Faludy accessible in English, a language in which, to his great disappointment as he once wrote me, he had not yet garnered many laurels.

Szerelmesversek egy haldoklóhoz:

IX.

Minden reggel sárgább és fáradtabb vagy.
Mikor fésüllek, törik a hajad.
Elszáradt inda a karod. Dagadnak
a rák gubói nyakadon. Az ablak
előtt kék ég, részvétlen szirtfalak.

Ma nem fáj semmid. Ülök ágyad mellett
s a kávéscsészét tartom. Hegyes melled
helyén zöld varrat, lila sebhelyek.
Ábrándozom, hogy nem kell még elmenned,
és egy fél évig veled lehetek.

Szerelmem, harmincnégy kilós kísértet,
mit mondjak néked? Áldom a napot,
mert pasztell-szürke szemeid még szépek,
mert roncs testedben van még egy kis élet,
s mert így is jó. S már nem lesz soha jobb.

Love Poems for Her, Dying

IX.

Each day you are more tired and more yellow.
I comb your hair, the shafts break like sere stalks.
Your arms are dried-out vines. The cancer's buboes
bulge out around your neck. Out of the window
blue sky, inexorable concrete walls.

Today there is no pain. Beside your bedstead
I hold your coffee cup. Your pointed breast
replaced by purple bruises, puckered green thread.
I muse that you need not be leaving just yet,
that I have a whole half-year with you left.

My love, seventy-five-pound wraith, my soul's wife,
what can I tell you? That I thank the Lord
because there is still beauty in your grey eyes,
because this wreck of you still holds some stray life,
that this is much. And never will be more.

Kis Képeskönyv:

Nagy Sándor, I.

A babiloni táj üres; az alkony
ragacs a friss makedón levegő
után. A sátorban boroznak, hosszú
asztal mellett. A középen, ez ő.
A nap nem tudta homloka fehérjét
kiszívni. Égszínkék madárszeme
nagy és merev. Az ajka kissé nyitva
s piheg, mint máskor is. Szemközt vele
Hepháisztion, aki hozzá hasonlít,
csak még szebb és még szőkébb a haja:
bűvös tükör, kiben önmagát látja,
mikor belenéz nappal s éjszaka.
Isznak. Másként hogy tudnák elviselni
fiatalságukat s a végtelen
győzelmeket? Dicsőségről beszélnek,
de senki sem mond semmi lényegest.
A lényeg ő. Itt bent mind őt imádják,
mint kint a katonák; varázsa már
a Balkántól a Hindukusig ér fel,
ahogy akarta. Néki nincs határ.
Miért? Zsenije, bátorsága számít?
Hogy jó volt, vagy rossz, az fel sem merül.
Három évezred világhódítói
közt ő maradt meg csak sértetlenül,—
megrohadtak mind: Szánherib, Hulágú,
a sakálhangú Hitler, Szolimán,
Rámzesz, Timúr, Dzsingisz, Sztálin, a sintér,—
Sándor márványa nem törik. Feláll

Little Picture Book:

Alexander the Great, I.

The Babylonian landscape is desolate; the twilight
a sticky sludge after the fresh air of Macedon.
They sit in the big tent, drinking
around the long table. The one in the middle is him.
The sun has not tarnished the white of his brow.
His eyes, greyish-blue, bird-like, large, rigid, motionless;
his lips, slightly parted, move imperceptibly
with each of his usual rapid, staccato breaths.
The one sitting facing him is Hephaestion, who is
similar to him, but even more golden, even more
beautiful. A magic mirror he consults night and day,
and meets there his own face, own soul.
They drink. Of course they drink; how else could they possibly
bear their own youth and endless victories?
They speak of honour and glory, but nobody
says anything essential, anything serious.
He is essential. Everyone in the tent worships him,
just as outside the soldiers do. His magic resonates
from down in the Balkans as far as the Hindu Kush,
as he had wanted. For him, there are no boundaries.
Why? Is it his courage, his genius—are these what matters?
If he was good, or bad? It makes no difference:
among the great conquerors of three millennia
he alone survives; intact, inviolate.
The rest have all rotted—Caesar, Sennacherib,
Stalin the butcher, Timur and Genghis,
Suleiman, Ramesses, the jackal-voiced Hitler—still,
Alexander's marble does not crack. He rises

az asztaltól s izzadtan a dermesztő
hegyi patakba ugrik fürdeni.
A társai aggódnak. Pedig tudják,
hogy a haláltól sem kell félteni.

from the table, and perspiring as he is,
throws himself into the cold mountain stream to bathe.
His companions worry, even though they all know
they need have no fear for him, not even of death.

Nagy Sándor, II.

Miért indult világhódító útra?
Hogy elkerüljön végre szörnyeteg
anyjától? Vagy hogy hírneve felérjen
Fülöp királyéval, kit megvetett?
Aligha. Vagy azért, amit Isszoszból
irt Dáreiosznak: hogy most bosszút áll
a perzsákon? De volt-e szükség erre
százhatvan év meg Máráthón után?
Vagy úgy igaz, ahogy ő maga mondta:
egy szenvedély hajtja, hogy túltegyen
Ákhilészen és oly nevet szerezzen,
mint előtte s utána senkisem?
Vagy ezt is a történetírók adták
szájába? Mert másként ki érti meg,
hogy egy maroknyi sereggel elindult
népek, folyók, sivatagok, hegyek
s két földrész ellen? Lehetett-e józan?
Félisten volt-e kívül és belül,
őrült kamasz, ki élvezte, hogy néki
a lehetetlen folyton sikerül?
Ugyan ki tud egy világbirodalmat
maga előtt úgy rugdosni, akár
a rongylabdát, ha számba vette egyszer,
hogy mi az élet és mi a halál?
Vagy a kíváncsiság vitte utazni
az Indusig? Kaland volt az egész,
s azért harcolt csak, mert útját elállták?
Vagy mindez téves, s Arisztótelész
volt felbujtója, mikor kioktatta
még otthon, hogy a földtányér kerek,

Alexander the Great, II.

Why did he set out to conquer the world? To get away
finally from his monstrous mother? Or that his name
might be equal to that of King Philip
whom he held in contempt?
Unlikely. Perhaps the reason is in the message he sent
to Darius from Issus, that he would now take revenge upon
the Persians? But was there a need for that
after a hundred and sixty years, and after Marathon?
Or does the truth lie in what he said himself,
that one passion, to outshine Achilles and to gain a name
like no-one before or after him,
was what drove him on?
Or was this, too, put in his mouth by the writers of history?
For how, otherwise, would it make any sense
that he set out with a handful of men against nations,
rivers, deserts, mountains, and two continents?
Can he have been sane? Was he half god, within
and without? A mad adolescent who enjoyed the fact
that he continually and always succeeded
against impossible odds?
For who would be able to boot and bunt
an empire before him just like a football, if
he had once stopped to think about
what life was, what death?
Or was it his fancy to travel as far as the Indus?
Was it all an adventure and did he do battle
merely because someone was always barring his way?
Or is all of this wrong, and it was Aristotle
who lit the fuse when he schooled him at home still
that the earth-disc was round as a platter, its rim

s India túlsó partján van a széle?
Ezért nyomult-e előre kelet
felé, míg katonái nemet mondtak,
hogy végül mégsem érje el, amit
akart: hogy a föld legszélén a semmi
fölé lógassa hosszú lábait?

on the far side of India?
Was this the reason he pressed ever eastward until his men
mutinied and refused to go on,
in the end to be denied his wish that from the very edge
of the world he might dangle
over the empty void his long, restless legs?

Csótány az íróasztalon*

Késő éjjel jön elő s íróasztalom lapján
megáll, a teáscsésze mögött vagy porcelán
hamutartómhoz lapul, vagy Fényes László képe
    alá bújik és onnan les ki rám.

Borzongok, ha áttetsző, undok testét kell látnom,
és hányszor próbáltam már agyoncsapni, de nem
sikerült. Ösztönei pompásak. Rögtön elfut,
    ha rávillan mozdulatlan szemem.

S hogyan szalad! Váratlan irányba, mindig másként,
olykor egyenest felém. Néha egy szökkenő
nagy ugrással eltűnik. Olykor egyik könyvembe
    rejtőzik és csak másnap jön elő.

Feladtam a küzdelmet. Tűröm, hogy antennáit
felém fordítsa s nézzen, alamuszi bogár.
De mit akar?—tűnődöm. Fogócskázni szeretne?
    Ingerel, kémlel, bámul, provokál?

Tanulni kíván? De mit? Fogalmakat nem ismer
azt se tudja, hogy él, hogy lábai száma hat
s körötte a mindenség. S nem érti, hogy most szemközt
    ülök s megírom őt és magamat.

És mégis mindent megsejt, ami lényeges néki.
Mióta nem akarom leütni, közelebb
húzódott. Izgatottan lengeti csápját, hogyha
    felállok s egy pohár tejért megyek,

---

* A csótányokra nem hat a nukleáris sugárzás.

The Cockroach on My Desk*

Late at night he creeps out, scuttles on my desk,
pauses by the teacup, darts round to the rear
of my ashtray, or László Fényes' portrait,
and peers at me from there.

I shudder at his body's disgusting, ugly gloss.
The times I've tried to strike him dead! Vain intent—
one flash from my unmoving eye—he's gone.
His instincts are magnificent.

And how he runs at unexpected tangents,
sometimes straight at me; then vanishing from sight,
hiding in a book, he may not reappear
until the following night.

Giving up the fight, I tolerate his gaze,
sly beetle, waggling his antennae at me.
I wonder what he wants? To spy? To play?
Admire, provoke, or tease?

To learn perhaps? But what? Concepts are beyond him:
that he goes on six legs, even that he lives,
the universe surrounds him—he can't even see
he is the he of this.

And yet he intuits all that concerns him.
Since I abandoned my intent to kill,
he's moved in closer; palps excitedly waving
when I go to fetch some milk;

---

* The cockroach is not affected by nuclear radiation.

de tejért és nem könyvért. Ha elfordulok, gyorsan
belekóstol s a csésze árnyékában megáll,
mohón vizsgál, nem mozdul. Sötét szeme tükrében
   látom magam. Mit akar, mire vár?

Azért figyel így engem, hogy emlékébe véssen?
Megsejtette, mi lesz most fajtámmal és velem,
mihelyt befejeződik az ezredes vérfürdő,
   mit úgy becézünk, hogy "történelem"?

Sajnál bennünket? tudná, hogy feladtuk magunkat,
sírjainkat, a várost, virágot, fát, mezőt,
s bolygónk sziklaágyáról a robbanás lerántja
   majd kérgét, mint a mocskos lepedőt?

Megérezte, hogy így lesz? Vagy én vetítettem ki
magamból ezt, mert tudom, hogy semmi sem marad,
s a romok alól csak ők jönnek elő sértetlen,
   a csótányok meg a svábbogarak?

Így végződnék örökre az ember rémuralma?
Félniök mérgeinktől s tőlünk majd sose kell,
és boltjaink beomlott bányáiban számukra
   évmilliókig akad eledel.

Csápjukat összefonják, látom: kartáncot járnak.
A semmi végtelenjén ők lesznek az urak.
Boldogság száll le rájuk. Szabadok végre s nyíltan
   hallathatják zizegő hangjukat.

Bölcsészetünk képzelgés volt, metafizikánk is.
És tudományunk vége: tömegsír, siralom.
A csótány néz és én őt. Hirtelenében elkap
   az indulat. Mégis agyoncsapom.

but milk, now, not a book. When I turn my back,
he tastes quickly, stops in the shadow of the cup, stares greedily,
but moves not. Dark mirror eyes:
I see myself. Now what?

Is he watching to commit me to memory?
Because he knows what awaits me and my kind
when the age-old bloodbath we call "history"
finally comes to an end?

Does he pity us? Knowing our race gave up
its towns, trees, fields and graves, even its very self?
That from earth's carcass an explosion will flay
the skin like a bloody pelt?

Can he see the future? Or do I project
my own thoughts upon him: that nothing will remain,
nothing crawl forth intact from the rubble
but the cockroach and his kin?

Will this be the way our grand tyranny ends?
They'll have no further need to fear our poisons,
and the caved-in mines of our shops will provide
food for them for aeons.

They link their antennae, form a chorus line,
new lords of the infinity of Nothing;
happiness descends on them, free to listen
openly to their own hissings.

Our wisdoms and our gods were only daydreams,
and so our knowledge: a mass grave for a bed.
We stare, the roach and I. Something seizes me
and I strike him dead.

EVAN JONES
TRANSLATES KIKI DIMOULA (Greek)

For English readers, the major and minor poets of Greece in the 20th century are male. Cavafy, Seferis, Elytis, and Ritsos have dominated the ideals of what Modern Greek poetry was and should be with their mythopoeic, Modernist visions of the world. The lack of major women poets began to be addressed in the 60s and 70s, when Kiki Dimoula (b. 1931) and other women came to prominence in Greece. But the kind of success earlier male poets achieved outside of the country – Nobel Prizes, prestigious foreign translations, general international interest in poetry – has evaded this generation of women poets. Reasons for this change in opportunity are easy to suggest, but the biggest one has been the growing gap between national cultures in our dissolving post-modern era: fewer poets reach out and so fewer are looking in.

Dimoula herself admitted in a 2000 interview that her own ambitions are so "limited to the domestic scene" that they barely extend beyond her own room, but this aspect of her poetics suggests humility rather than hermeticism. In Greece, her individual collections sell regularly in the area of ten thousand copies and she has twice won the State Prize for Poetry; as well, in 2003, she became the first woman elected to the Chair in Poetry at the Academy of Athens. But the domesticity that is so central to her is cause for suspicion in some circles. One notable Greek poet called her a "housewife" in conversation with me, inferring a place for her work in a sort of literary scene addressed – authentically or not – by Oprah's Book Club in North America. That her poems present themselves within domestic spaces does link her to this, but the dynamism in her syntax tells of something else: the quality of her verse, yes, but also her need to construct the world in new and surprising ways, to jump zeugmatically "from the branches of trees and senses / into the branches of trees and senses." This is what remains the most attractive feature in her poems: their attention to the adventure in the development of the quotidian.

In translating these four poems, I have tried to avoid "undercooking" them, in Michael Hofmann's sense, and leaving them too literal sounding, but also to maintain some of Greek grammar's foreign-ness – thus not accommodating the poems to English, but accommodating English to the poems. The result, I hope, reveals Dimoula's unique tone and voice without too much of my own mark.

Δεν ξέρω αν θα 'ρθω αύριο

Στο διπλανό σπίτι κάποιος μαθαίνει πιάνο.
Αρχάριος ακόμα, νοερά τον διδάσκω
τη μουσική αξία του επαναλαμβανόμενου.

Έπαιζα κι εγώ κάποτε πλήκτρα
αλλά μόνο μεταξύ στενοτάτων κύκλων.
Σε τίποτα βαφτίσια ανησυχίας
κανένα γάμο βιαστικά εγκύου πάλι
ελπίδας με πολύφρενο ίσως
και σε πανηγύρια πολιούχων χωρισμών.

Δίπλα ο μαθητής δεν φαίνεται τόσο ερασιτέχνης.
Κάθε μεσημέρι επίμονα ασκείται στη μονοτονία.
Οι ίδιες νότες στις ίδιες σκάλες
ηδύτατα επανέρχεται
της επανάληψης η υπόγεια μελωδία.

Κάθε μεσημέρι ανεφοδιάζει ο μαθητής
της μνήμης μου την κλίμακα
με υποτιμημένη επιστροφή θείας μονοτονίας:

Πρώτα της κάτω πόρτας το νιαούρισμα
– η σκουριασμένη δοξαριά του μεντεσέ της –
ύστερα τα βήματα στις ίδιες νότες των σκαλιών
– διακριτικά μην και προϊδεάσεις
την πολύ ευέξαπτη μαρμάρινη υφή τους –
και με το πενάκι του κλειδιού
να προανακρούεις την άφιξη και να δονείς
τα τέλια της εισόδου σου στο σπίτι.
Κάθε μεσημέρι . Στό κάθε *κάθε*.

I Don't Know If I'll Be Here Tomorrow

In the house next door someone is learning piano.
Still a beginner, I teach him psychically
the musical value of repetition.

I also played the keys once
but only for special occasions.
At restless christenings
or weddings rushed into because of pregnancy
—a hope there for well-endowment perhaps—
and at festivals for separations' patron saints.

Next door the student doesn't appear so amateurish.
Each midday he practices incessantly in monotone.
The same notes in the same scales
return sweetly
the interwall melody of repetition.

Each midday the student of my memory
provides the scale
with underestimated return and divine monotones:

First the mewing of the door below
—the rusted bows of its hinges—
later the steps to the same notes of the scale
—discreetly, as you are not prepared for
their irritable marble texture—
and with the little pen of the key
you introduce the arrival and vibrate
the strings of your entry into the house.
Each midday. At every *each*.

Μιά μουσική πού όσο παίζεται
αμελείς ν' ακούς όπως δεν ακούς το ψωμί
όταν ζυγώνει κάθε μέρα την προϋπόθεση σου
όπως ουδέποτε προσέχεις
τη μέρα όταν φεύγοντας κάθε φορά σου λέει
δέν ξέρω αν θα 'ρθω αύριο.
Δεν την ακούς καί παραλείπεις
να πείς μισό ευχαριστώ
σ' αυτή τη μέρα που ήρθε και αύριο ωστόσο
παρά τη βασιμή της επιφύλαξη που διέτρεχες.

Με τον καιρό
χάνει το μουσικό αυτί της η συνήθεια
λεωφόρος φάλτσα το κελάρυσμά της.
Το καθημερινό σιγά σιγά απελπίζεται
πως είναι αιώνιο – άρρωστο –
τρέχει σε κομπογιανίτες γάμους πανηγύρια
να γιάνει τάχα πίνοντας εφήμερο νερό.

Κάθεται η μονότονη επανάληψη στο πιάνο
όταν κοιμόμαστε η λείπουμε να γράψει
τα μελωδικά απομνημονεύματά της.
Τα υστερόφημα.

A music that plays so long that
you neglect to hear it as you don't hear bread
as far as you're concerned being kneaded daily
as you never notice
the day when it's leaving each night saying to you
I don't know if I'll be here tomorrow.
You don't hear it and you never
say half a thank you
to this day which came and will do the same tomorrow
despite its well-founded reserve which you ran through.

With time
the habit will lose its musical ear
the mistaken avenue of its burbling.
Little by little it fears daily
that it's eternal—ill—
flowing in charlatans and marriages and festivals
as if to heal by the drinking of ephemeral water.

The monotonous repetition sits at the piano
while we sleep or are away writing
its melodic memoir.
The post-fame.

Εύφημος μνεία στην αφάνεια

Φαίνονται πούλμαν εκδρομικά στο βάθος
παρκαρισμένα κατά μήκος τοιχίου αισθητού.
Περιφράσσει διασήμων προσώπων
τη θαμμένη αθανασία που ήθελες
σώνει και καλά να επισκεφτείς – μελαγχόλησες
βλέποντας κι εδώ εις την ξένην να είναι
πιασμένες όλες οι θέσεις της φήμης.

Καθισμένος πολύ μακριά από το φυσικό σου μέγεθος.
Φαίνεσαι σαν κομπάκι που έχει στην άκρη
το κοτσάνι των μεγάλων φύλλων – έπεσαν
σ' επίστρωση σχολαστική γύρω από τη θέση σου
και πέρα –
σαν ρόζος στον κορμό του δέντρου που ακουμπάς.

Είναι που σε γνωρίζω διά παντός
και καταφέρνει κάπως ν' αναγνωρίζεται
πόσο αγαπώ ποιός είσαι.
Αλλιώς θα έμενε άγνωστο
αφανές κι αυτό.

Honourable Mention in Obscurity

Tour buses arrived in the background,
parking along the length of the tangible wall,
fencing off the famous faces,
the buried immortality that you sought
exhausted. Good thing you came—though
it saddened you, for in this strange locale
all the places of fame are taken.

Seated so far from your natural greatness,
you appeared like a tiny growth that has at one end
the stems of thick leaves—fallen
into pedantic covering around your place
and beyond—
like a knot in the tree trunk that you rested against.

It's where I know all about you
and somehow it knows
that I love who you are.
Otherwise it would remain unknown,
invisible and your own.

Ζούγκλα

Πρωί κι όλα του κόσμου
στημένα
στην ιδεώδη απόσταση μιάς μονομαχίας.
Τα όπλα έχουν διαλεχτεί,
τα ίδια πάντα,
οι ανάγκες σου, οι ανάγκες μου.
Αυτός που θα μέτραγε *ένα, δύο, τρία, πυρ*
καθυστερούσε,
κι ώσπου να 'ρθεί
καθίσαμε στην ίδια *καλημέρα*
και χαζεύαμε τη φύση.

Η εξοχή βρισκότανε στην ήβη
και το πράσινο ασελγούσε.
Κραυγές τροπαιοφόρου θηριωδίας
έσερνε ο Ιούνιος της υπαίθρου.
Πιανόταν και πηδούσε
από κλαδί δέντρων κι αισθήσεων
σε κλαδί δέντρων κι αισθήσεων,
Ταρζάν ταινίας μικρού μήκους
που κυνηγάει αθέατα θηρία
στη μικρή ζούγκλα μιάς ιστορίας.
Το δάσος υποσχότανε πουλιά
και φίδια.
Δηλητηριώδης αφθονία αντιθέτων.
Το φως έπεφτε καταπέλτης
σ' ό,τι δεν ήταν φως,
κι η ερωτομανής λαμπρότης
παράφορα φιλούσε κι ό,τι δεν ήταν έρωτας,
μέχρι και τη δική σου συνοφρύωση.

Jungle

Morning and people the world over
initiate
a duel at the ideal range.
The weapons are chosen,
always the same,
your needs versus my needs.
He who will count to three and shout *fire!*
is late,
and until he comes
we sit in the same *good morning*
and gaze at nature.

The pubescent countryside
is debauched but green.
June lets out ferocious cries
of victory into the open air.
Touched, it jumps
from the branches of trees and senses
into the branches of trees and senses,
like short films
where Tarzan chases invisible animals
through the small jungle of a story.
The forest promises birds
and snakes.
Poisonous abundance of contradiction.
The light falls catapult-like
in that it isn't light,
and the brilliant love-sick woman
kisses furiously and it isn't love,
as your own frown divulges.

Στη μικρή εκκλησία άλλος κανείς
εκτός από το πολύ ονομά της, *Ελευθερώτρια.*
Ένας Χριστός περίφροντις
μέτραγε με το πάθος του φιλάργυρου
το βίος του:
καρφιά κι αγκάθια.
Επόμενο ήταν να μην έχει ακούσει
τους πυροβολισμούς.

At the small church, no others
despite its name being *Libertina*.
A concerned Christ there
counts the passions of his miserly
life: nails and thorns.
He won't hear
the gunfire that comes next.

Διάλογος ανάμεσα σε μένα και σε μένα

Σου είπα:
– Λύγισα.
Και είπες:
– Μη θλίβεσαι.
Απογοητεύσου ήσυχα.
Ήρεμα δέξου να κοιτάς
σταματημένο το ρολόι.
Λογικά απελπίσου
πως δεν είναι ξεκούρδιστο,
ότι έτσι δουλεύει ο δικός σου χρόνος.
Κι αν αίφνης τύχει
να σαλέψει κάποιος λεπτοδείκτης,
μη ριψοκινδυνέψεις να χαρείς.
Η κίνηση αυτή δεν θα 'ναι χρόνος.
Θα 'ναι κάποιων ελπίδων ψευδορκίες.
Κατέβα σοβαρή,
νηφάλια αυτοεκθρονίσου
από τα χίλια σου παράθυρα.
Για ένα *μήπως* τ' άνοιξες.
Κι αυτοξεχάσου εύχαρις,
Ό,τι είχες να πεις,
για τα φθινόπωρα, τα ερώτων,
την αλληλοκτονία των ωρών,
των αγαλμάτων τη φερεγγυότητα,
ό,τι είχες να πεις
γι' ανθρώπους που σιγά σιγά λυγίζουν,
το είπες.

Dialogue Between Me and Myself

I said to you:
I relent.
And you said:
Don't be upset.
Be disappointed in silence.
Accept to look at
the stopped watch calmly.
Despair logically
that it is not unwound,
that your own time works this way.
And if suddenly a particular
minute-hand happens to move,
don't risk being happy.
This movement won't be time.
It will be fabrications of certain of your hopes.
Come down seriously,
dethrone yourself soberly
from your thousand windows,
which you opened for one *he*,
and let yourself go.
What you had to say,
to those autumns, the swans,
memory, the gutters of loves,
the statues' reliability,
what you had to say
to the men who slowly relented,
you said it.

SONNET L'ABBÉ
TRANSLATES KO UN (Korean)

I spent two non-consecutive years teaching in universities in South Korea, and learned the language at a basic level. I chose to work in Korean rather than French, my second language, because it stretched me further, brought my imagination outside of Canada, allowed me to relive the amazing experience of getting to know and love modern South Korea and in some ways was just more fun than sticking to a Western language. I love the challenge of a totally different syntax, of reading words written in an entirely different "alphabet," the strange way the visualness of Hangul is both foreign and yet accessible to me. Hangul calls to me like a secret doorway held wide open to another form of thought.

I experienced South Korea as a much more systemically patriarchal culture than ours. Gender and power relations are written right into the grammar of the language, and I often wonder if and how women's struggles for recognition in academic, literary and other professional spheres continue to be limited by the language's structural resistance to dehierarchization. So I first decided I would translate one of the best Korean female poets. According to Kim Hye-sun, "to live as a woman in Korea, and especially as a woman poet, is to endure many things... to occupy a marginal place, a mere spice within a world of poetry constructed by men." The struggles women face in South Korea for every kind of political voice were reflected in the difficulty I had in getting my hands on any of their work, the uneven quality of the work I did see, and the ultimate failure of my attempts to reach Kim Hye-Sun and the few other Korean women poets I tried to contact.

Were it not for these frustrated first attempts I might not have found the courage to approach Ko Un to translate the poems that appear here, which are from *Poems Left Behind* (Changbi, 2002). Ko Un is such a force in Korean literature and so well respected and translated worldwide that I was more than a little intimidated to propose this collaboration. However, my first inquiry was warmly and positively received by Lee Sang Wha, his wife and translator, with whom I have consulted on these poems.

A poet, essayist, novelist, translator and literary critic, Ko Un is generally acknowledged to be Korea's foremost contemporary writer. Allan Ginsberg has described him as "a magnificent poet, combined of Buddhist cognoscente, passionate political libertarian, and natural historian." Winner of the 2008 Griffin Lifetime Achievement Award and considered "a great mountain peak" by his Korean peers, he has written over 130 books. His poems range from tiny, haikuesque "flowers of a moment" to thousand-line epics, and reflect the history of his life as a dissident, prisoner and former Buddhist monk.

In these translations I have attempted to capture the "toughmindedness" and "raggedness" that Robert Hass has described as qualities of Ko Un's work, which I understand as its aesthetically loose yet syntactically spare diction, which are themselves part of a Korean poetic style that still shows the influence of its oral traditions. Reading Ko Un in translation has introduced me to an entirely new voice and aesthetic that combines wisdom with occasional stridence, humour with despair, and profundity with a light mindfulness that remains unclinging to its subjects.

I am indebted to Jihee Han at UBC for his invaluable help, particularly in distinguishing 웅덩이 from 엉덩이.

가고 싶은 곳

년 전
가고 싶은 곳이 있었습니다
백만분의 일 세계지도 모든 곳에
내가 가 있었습니다
년 전
꼭 가고 싶은 곳이 있었습니다
옥방 철창 사이로
푸른 하늘은 돌아쳐 나의 길이었습니다

그동안 몇군데는 터벅터벅 갈 수 있었습니다

그러나 몇군데는 그대로 남겨두었습니다
내가 이 세상 그만두어버린 뒤
내가 가고 싶은 그곳들이
누군가를 내내 기다릴 것입니다

가고 깊은 곳이 있었습니다
지는 꽃
지는 꽃 저녁 가슴 여며 눈감았습니다

Places I Want to Go

Thirty years ago
there were places I wanted to go.
I was going
everywhere on a one-millionth world map.
Twenty years ago
there were places I had to go.
Through the bars of my prison cell
the blue sky was my path.

Meanwhile I've been able to plod to some places.

And yet I left some places.
After I quit this world
the places I want to go
will keep waiting for someone.

There were places I wanted to go.
Falling flowers.
Falling flowers evening touches my heart I close my eyes.

아시아의 작은 산들

아시아 일백년의 굴욕은 의무였다
이제 다 뱉어라
주역 팔괘
묵은 가래 탁 뱉어라
저만치 웅덩이 한복판 과녁에 적중할 터
이어서
나의 근대 아닌 남의 근대 내버려라

돌아다보아라

대히말라야산맥을 누가 모르겠느냐
쿤룬산맥을
알타이산맥을 누가 모르겠느냐
그 산들의 혁혁한 이름
그것은
이제 산의 이름이 아니라
어떤 지상(至上)이었다
웅장함
위대함
그리고 숭고함이다

그러나 오늘 나는 그것을 배반하고
아시아 각 지역의 작은 산들에게 절하고 싶다
대히말라야에서는
천미터 이하의 산에는
좀처럼 이름을 붙이지 않는다
그러나 나는
1천미터 이하의 산들에게
수많은 산들에게
지는 해 넘어간 뒤 하나씩 외경의 이름 부르며 절하고
싶다

Asia's Small Mountains

Asia has been responsible to its hundred years of shame.
Spit it all out!
The I Ching, its eight trigrams.
Spit that stale phlegm right out!
Aim to hit the bull's eye of a puddle
then ditch
not my modernity, but man's.

Look around.

Who doesn't know the great Himalayas?
The Kunlun mountains,
the Altaic range, who doesn't know them?
These mountains' glorious names.
These names
are not the names of the mountains
but were a sort of superiority
majesty
might
and sublime.

Today I betray them.
I want to bow one by one to each of Asia's small mountains.
In the Himalayas
mountains less than eight thousand metres
are rarely given names.
But I want to bow
after the sunset
to the mountains less than a thousand metres high,
to all those mountains
calling out, one by one, each of their awesome names.

아시아 각 지역에서는
예로부터 앞산이 있다
내 소원이 있고
내 자식의 내일이 있다
월의 못 견디는 산록이 있다
앞산에는

아시아 사람에게는
뒷산이 있다
뒷산에는 조상의 무덤이 있다
빈 너도밤나무 가지들 밤새도록 흔들리고 있다
아열대
열대
그 일대에는 치렁치렁 장발의 그늘이 내려와 있다

웅장함도
위대함도
숭고함도 없이
아시아 각 지역 이름없는 작은 산들 찾아다니며
늙어가고 싶다
하나씩 이름 부르며 죽어가고 싶다
무능의 회한 다 바쳐
신새벽 쪽빛 하늘 내려와 있는
작은 산기슭에서
마지막으로 절하고 싶다

작은 산들이여
작은 산들이여 순이산이여 정희산이여
아시아의 진짜 이념의 집들이여 칠성이여 삼룡이여

Every Asian region
has had a mountain just in front of a house.
My wish,
my children's tomorrows,
the unbearable green of the mountainside in May
in the mountain facing my house.

Asian people have
the back mountains.
In these back mountains are our ancestors' graves.
The bare branches of beeches are trembling.
Subtropics,
tropics:
the shadow of long hair is unfurling over those regions.

Though not superior
majestic
or sublime
I want to grow old
looking for the nameless small mountains
of every Asian region.
I want to die
calling each and every one of their names.
As the new dawn's indigo sky
falls to the feet of the small mountains
I want to bow, finally,
offering up all my regret at my incompetence.

O small mountains!
Small mountains! Soon-i mountains! Jong-hui mountains!
Homes of Asia's true ideology! Great Bear! Three Dragons!

넋

풍뎅이였습니다
나방이었습니다
청솔귀뚜라미였습니다
오로지 불빛이라면 마구 달려갔습니다
죽은 뒤로는 새로 와서 처음 이빨 나는 아기였고
밤새 뒤척여 지새우는 파도들이었습니다 그 시절의
너는 그리고 나는

soul

were a May beetle
were a moth
were a green pine cricket
rushed blindly into any firelight
after death I returned as a baby with its first tooth and
all night the sleepless waves tossed and turned back then
you and I

A.F. MORITZ
TRANSLATES JUAN RAMÓN JIMÉNEZ (Spanish)

Juan Ramón Jiménez (1881-1958; Nobel Prize in literature, 1956) was born in the village of Moguer in Andalucia, southern Spain. His first books, published in 1900, contributed greatly to the establishment of a new literature in Spain. He, Miguel de Unamuno and Antonio Machado were the finest Spanish poets of the first third of the century, and Jiménez above the others exercised decisive influence, raising the level of Spanish culture in general, and shaping the famous generation of 1927: Federico García Lorca, Jorge Guillén, Vicente Aleixandre, Pedro Salinas, Rafael Alberti, Luis Cernuda and others. Under threat during the Spanish Civil War (1936-39), he emigrated to the United States, living and teaching in Maryland and Florida before settling in Puerto Rico. In 1956 Jiménez received word of his Nobel Prize almost simultaneously with the death of his wife, Zenobia. He did not recover from her loss and died in 1958.

Jiménez's work falls into three phases. The first, up to about 1915, is a creatively modernized version of late romanticism. The English-language reader can form some idea of it by imagining a poet who has written several books, already a life's work, in a manner parallel to that of Yeats' best poems before 1910. After 1915, Jiménez was one of the chief originators of the new, stripped, eliptical style and form that was introduced into European literature by the Imagists, the middle-period Yeats, and Pound and Eliot, by Ungaretti in Italy, and by Apollinaire, Cendrars, Reverdy and others in France. Jiménez's version of this is wholly his own, intensifying the penetration of earlier concerns by paradoxical means of a complete breach in manner. The third period belongs to the twenty-two years of his exile in America. It produced the long poem, *Space*, equal in quality and importance to the long poems of Pound, Eliot, Paz and Neruda; *God Desired and Desiring*, a sequence of mystical poems worthy of comparison with St. John of the Cross; and several collections containing many short poems of unexcelled beauty.

One characteristic of Jiménez's poetry difficult to translate is that, while the genius of his thought is universal, the genius of his style is organically and originally Spanish, as for instance is that of Emily Dickinson, whose work Jiménez loved and translated well, in English. A different difficulty comes from the way in which his utter originality contradicts the basic "no ideas but in things" shibboleth of modernism. He exalts music as the expression of feeling, feeling and thought above the image, and the image above descriptive detail, correctly locating the specificity and concreteness of the poem not in realities to which it refers but in its own specific, concrete embodiment of its creative impulse. Paz excellently says that Jiménez conceived the poem as exclamation, that is to say, a pure cry of recognition, love or lament, pleasure or pain.

Tristeza

Un día, vendrá un hombre
que, echado sobre ti, te intente desnudar
de tu luto de ignota,
¡palabra mía, hoy tan desnuda, tan clara!;
un hombre que te crea
sombra hecha agua de murmullo raro,
¡a ti, voz mía, agua
de luz sencilla!

Sadness

One day, my words, a man will come
and throw himself on you, meaning
to strip you naked, to tear off
your widow's weeds of dark obscurity.
My words, completely naked and clear today,
this man who is coming will see you as a shadow
that has turned into water with a strange
rarified murmur—yes, you, my voice,
you, water of simple light.

[Sin título]

Las cosas dan a luz. Yo
las amo, y ellas, conmigo,
en arcoiris de gracia,
me dan hijos, me dan hijos.

[Untitled] ·

Things give birth. I
love them. They
through a rainbow of grace
give me children, give me children.

Mariposa Malva

–¡Ahí va!
        –¡La primavera nueva!

Corren todos un punto, mudos, ciegos,
locos, sin saber qué era,
solo porque gritaron:
¡Ahí va la primavera nueva!

Y todos vuelven tristes,
caminando hacia atrás, sonriendo al frente,
con los brazos tendidos
y las manos abiertas.

–¡Qué lástima!
        –¡Sí era!
                Corren todos
de aquí a allá, ciegos, mudos,
locos, entre los secos árboles,
sobre las viejas hojas secas,
solo porque gritaron:
                ¡Si era!

Cruje todo el invierno, exhala
olores de madera seca y tierra
abierta.
        –¡Ay, ay, ay, ay!
                Todos miran

Mauve Butterfly

There she goes,
         the new season, the spring.

They all set off, mute and blind, addled,
not knowing what it was, running,
only because they themselves had shouted,
There goes the newborn spring.

And they all return unhappy,
walking backwards, smiles on their faces,
with arms stretched out
and hands open.

Too bad.
         It really was her.
                     They all run
here and there, blind and mute,
addled, through the bare trees
over the old dry leaves
only because they themselves shouted,
                     It's really her...

The whole winter creaks, exhaling
odours of naked wood
and open earth.
                 Ay, ay, ay, ay!
                     They all look

al cielo, abriendo inmensa-
mente los ojos, olvidados
de la tarde.

     Y caen, al fin, mustios,
como una yerba muerta
quemada de ansia. Al lado de su sueño,
la mariposa malva se ha quedado quieta.

up at the sky, holding their eyes
hugely open, entirely forgetting
this late afternoon.

And finally they collapse, wilted,
like a dead blade of grass burnt
by worry and want. Beside their dream
the mauve butterfly rests quiet.

Tarde

¡Qué lejos llegan, en tu azul, silencio,
sin esos golpes agrios que las hacen
plegarse, sensitivas,
las alas de mi frente!
Se diría
que no van a volver nunca ya a mí.

—Recuerdo
los barriletes de las tardes de mi infancia,
con el mareo precursor
del cielo en que ellos agitados revolaban,
yo en sombra, ellos con sol...—

Late mi corazón, como una madre
que va a quedarse sin su hijo; como
una doncella que va a ser esposa.
¡Oh misterioso miedo
que hace encojerse el cuerpo al alma,
como para ponerle
con ella contrapeso a lo infinito;
miedo gustoso, que no quiere
hacer volver las alas que se van,
ni quedarse sin ellas;
miedo de lo que ven, de lo que saben;
de verlo —¡y qué deleite!– de saberlo!

¡Oh miedo misterioso
de la belleza diaria no sabida!

Early Evening

How far, silence, the wings of my thinking go
into your blue, free up there from the angry
buffetings that make them,
in their sensitivity, fold.
Now it almost seems
they'll never come back to me.

I remember
the barrel-kites in the early evenings
of my childhood as they bucked
and spun on the sky's prophetic tides—
me down in darkness, them close to the sun.

My heart beats hard, it's like a mother
whose child is leaving home, it's like a young
woman on her way to be married.
Mysterious fear,
which moves the body to lock the soul inside,
as if that way it could turn her
into a counterweight against the infinite.
Joyful fear, which cannot bear
to make the wings that have flown come back
and cannot bear to stay here without them.
Fear of what those wings are seeing, what they know,
and yet, delight at seeing it, delight in knowing.

Mysterious fear
of each day's beauty never understood.

Humo y Oro

¡Tanto mar con luna amarilla
entre los dos, España! —y tanto mar, mañana sol del alba...—

        ...Parten,
entre la madrugada, barcos vagos,
cuyas sirenas tristes, cual desnudas,
oigo, despierto, despedirse
—la luna solitaria
se muere, rota ¡oh Poe! sobre Broadway—.
oigo despierto, con la frente
en los cristales yertos; oigo
despedirse una vez y otra, entre el sueño
—a la aurora no queda más que un hueco
de fría luz en donde hoy estaba
la negra mole ardiente—,
entre el sueño de tantos como duermen
en su definitiva vida viva
y al lado
de su definitiva vida muerta...

      ¡Qué lejos, oh qué lejos
de ti y de mí y de todo, en esto
—los olivares de la madrugada—,
al oír la palabra alerta—¡muerte!—
dentro de la armonía de mi alma
—mar inmenso de duelo o de alegría—,
a la luz amarilla
de esta luna poniente y sola, España!

Smoke and Gold

So much sea with its yellow moon between us,
my Spain—and so much sea tomorrow with the rising sun.

                Vague shipping
departs into the pre-dawn hour
and awake I listen to its sad
as-though-naked horns sounding goodbye—
the solitary moon
is dying over Broadway, broken (Poe!)—
awake I listen with my head against
the unyielding windowpane; I listen
to goodbye over and over, in the dream
(the sunrise is nothing now but a hollow
shape of cold light where earlier today
stood a black, ardent bulk)...
in the dream of how many who sleep it would seem
in their life definitively alive
at the side
of their definitively living death.

       How far away
from you, me, and everything this is—
from your olive groves in the pre-dawn hour—
as I listen to the warning word—death—
in the harmony of my soul, a sea
of pain and happiness, immense,
in the yellow light,
my Spain, of this moon going down alone.

Cielo

Se me ha quedado el cielo
en la tierra, con todo lo aprendido,
cantando, allí.
                        Por el mar este
he salido a otro cielo, más vacío
e ilimitado como el mar, con otro
nombre que todavía
no es mío como es suyo...
                        Igual que, cuando
adolescente, entré una tarde
a otras estancias de la casa mía
–tan mía como el mundo–,
y dejé, allá junto al jardín azul y blanco,
mi cuarto de juguetes, solo
como yo, y triste...

Sky

I left my sky
singing back there on land
with everything I've learned.
                And through this sea
I went out under another sky, more empty,
limitless like the sea, and bearing some other
name, its own, that still is not
a name to me...
                It's like that evening
in adolescence when I came across
other regions of my house,
which is mine the same way the world is,
and I left, down by the white
and sky-blue garden, my room full of toys
alone like me and grieving.

ERÍN MOURE
TRANSLATES *CHUS PATO* (Galician)

"Animality and language": An introductory note

In bringing Chus Pato's words into English, the translator has to travel at breakneck speed, trying not to trip over the tree roots and go flying. I still end up with skinned knees. Pato topples all lyric convention in a rush of grammatical continuity/ discontinuity to bring us face to face (kiss or collide!) with the traumas and migrations of Western European history, writing itself, and the possibility (or not) of poetry accounting for our animal selves: our selves who will die.

The urgency of her task is such that Pato wriggles out of any known form of the poem, and out of the confines of the book. The poems translated here are from *Hordes of Writing*, the third volume in her projected pentology *Method*, in which she refashions the way we think of the possibilities of the poetic text, of words, of bodies, of political and literary space, and of the construction of ourselves as individual, community, nation, world.

"I wanted to write a book that did not derive its structural unity from free verse, but from a horde of words: a protective mechanism borne deep inside it, but with maximum freedom, and mobility," says Pato. "The horde is the mode of perfect human relation because it is the perfect protected space for human beings, like the mother's womb. It also makes us think of constant movement, mobility like that of the barbarians, with their absolute freedom."

Chus Pato comes from a very literate culture (think of the riches of the medieval cantigas), albeit one small in numbers, that flourishes despite being under siege, yet it passes almost unperceived by readers in English. I think it critical to my own culture to bring discomfiting – and exhilarating – work such as Pato's into Canadian literature, to perturb us and upend our views of writing's possibilities.

Her work returns freedom to us, not that of the individual speaking from an illusory autonomy constructed on the invisibility of others, but the freedom to be an organism among others and receive others as organisms, migrants, blastulæ, lives. "The poet is he or she whose muse has been integrally destroyed," writes Pato. But there is always a remnant, she says, and from this remnant the poet picks up the pen again, and keeps writing.

"Rather than letting the world into my writing," says Pato, "I kick writing out into the world." Her works – such shock mechanisms – have made her one of the most revered figures in Galician literature.

Como moitos dos seus compañeir@s fora adestrada na ana-
corese e no delirio. Eu era un lugar baleiro, así pois Eu era un
lugar que só podería ser substituído por afecto: de non ser así, Eu
sería destruído.

Irrompes desde o sentido

non o cubras, trénzao
trenza o que nunca poderás dicir
etrénzao co xeo, co alento dos humanos, coa árbore, co río.

Os signos son indiferentes pero soñan e aparéanse
a razón é menos veloz
do lado que fala acumulamos catástrofes

naturalmente estamos no xardín, nunha dimensión de cobertura,
e todas as artes que se derivan da luz—a pintura, as cintas fílmicas
e a carne—son anteriores á voz. Entón sería unha escritura com-
posta de significantes radicais; teriamos un texto descendido dos
procesos lumínicos, os telefilmes, o soño e a cópula. De contado
todós estariamos non-vestidos, non-espidos e os nosos nomes
serían instantáneos cos suxeitos

os ollos fatigados (cegos) apenas discirnen
dita

«(...) malia o que moitos cren non se rexistra contigüidade entre
poema e delirio, sustentándose este último nunha estrutura narra-
tiva. De buscarlle semellanza, elixiría as series televisivas. Un suxeito
delirante arranca dun eu (sería máis exacto empregar a cifra menos-
eu) que non puido conectarse debidamente a ningún romance de
familia, sometido a unha violencia extrema

Like many of her compatriots she'd been trained in anachoresis and delirium. *I* was an empty site, therefore *I* was a site that could only be substituted by affect: otherwise, *I* would be destroyed.

You burst in from meaning

you don't get it, you weave it
weave what you'd never be able to say
and weave it with ice, with human breath, with tree, river.

Signs are indifferent but dream and copulate
reason is slower
from the side that speaks we accumulate catastrophes

naturally we're in the garden, in a protected dimension, and all arts derived from light—painting, film and flesh—precede the voice. Thus it'd be a writing composed of radical signifiers; our text would stem from luminous processes, telefilms, dream and copulation. We'd all be quickly nonclothed, non-naked and our names instantaneously subjects

the eyes, tired (blind) scarcely discern
dictate:

"(...) despite what many believe, no contiguity registers between poem and delirium, the latter shored up in a narrative structure. If you want a comparison, try television series. A delirious subject start off in an I (it would be more exact to use the term less-I) that couldn't connect properly to any family romance, submitted to an extreme violence

son de gloria as auras do delirio, incitadas a unha permanente
resurrección, corpos de apocalipse

calquera pequeno roedor, cando se estresa, delira.

O sexo é unha escena de luz

así o que chamamos intimidade

son labios, verdadeiramente bolboretas.

•

Eu está no xeo e na mañá
Eu está no alento do río e na mañá

o meu nome // na árbore.

they're glorious, the auras of delirium, incited to permanent
resurrection, bodies of the apocalypse

any small rodent, under stress, is delirious,

Sex is a scene of light

thus what we call intimacy

are lips, real butterflies.

•

I is in the ice and in morning
I is in river mist and in morning

my name // incised in the tree.

Non tanto o tema sobre o que le *(a soberanía é o punto de indifer-*
enza entre violencia e dereito) senón a forma expositiva que afecta
ao debate

faina feliz

como a montaña, as árbores, a beleza.

De novo os campos de aviación, as equipaxes perdidas
como se quedase para sempre aí, nunha relación de pertenza e
non inclusión
noutro continente

fóra de bando
fóra de bandeira

nunha banda de lobas (abandonada), de bandidas, que son sen-
tido, un revólver en cada voz.

As docas ciclónicas no Atlántico sur

as ondas cúbicas
pois iso son (o pai chegou anos despois, non coñecía aos netos,
non sabía prender o dvd nin os outros aparatos electrónicos da
casa)
unha labrega que cruza o océano e cen anos despois escribe.

En realidade, en determinados momentos da vida le constante
o mesmo libro: unha narración de versións invariábeis; trata
sobre os deuses, os augures e as tumbas; as frases non a fan
avanzar, ningunha fe a exalta

It's not so much the subject she reads about (*sovereignty is the zone of indifference between violence and law*) but its expositional form that affects the debate

it makes her glad

like mountain, trees, beauty.

The airfields again, baggage lost
as if she's stuck there forever in a relation of belonging and non-inclusion
on another continent

outside the flock
outside the flag

in a pack of she-wolves (abandoned), of she-bandits who are meaning, a revolver in each voice.

The indolent low-pressure zones of the south Atlantic

the cubic waves,
that's what they are (the father arrived years later, didn't know the grandchildren, or how to use the DVD or any other home electronics)
a farmwoman who crosses the ocean and, a century later, writes.

In reality, at certain points of her life, she rereads the same book: a narration of invariable versions; it's about gods, omens and tombs; the sentences don't lead her forward, no faith exalts her

cando experimenta a éxtase amorosa, a violencia do rapto—
constitutiva e tan imprecisa coma un remuíño de neve, un enxame
de abellas ou a pálida luz dun facho inunda aos deuses, aos augur-
ios e ás tumbas—, entón o pracer—unha caverna remota, unha
néboa escura, azul, cincenta, gris como un Himalaia—talla as
letras na trama do papiro

esa gruta, esa tebra e os xemidos do gozo articulan a forza do que
se desata no idioma

Como a masa que estiramos co rolo e que finalmente ocupa unha
xeometría completa, como a maraña de gromos

son consistentes os corpos, establecen sentido.

O que trato de aclarar é que, malia a súa configuración xeminal,
o corte autorial non pode coincidir, nin se inclina cara a
ningunha das dúas series contrapostas. Con todo, dado que o
poema só se inscribe alí onde é imposíbel a súa concreción
(fóra do arquivo e do xa rexistrado) non pode serlle fiel a
ningunha das tres categorías descritas. Talvez por esta causa os
insectos, as aves e certas criaturas mitolóxicas (vitorias, amores
e a mensaxeira dos deuses, así como as xerarquías anxélicas)
son alíferas.

Aínda que o tramo anterior privilexia o símil «unha columna
de bolboretas», sería igualmente factíbel o gran canón do Sil e
as súas ribeiras, así como a balanza de Osiris

(as tres comparacións salientadas non esgotan nin moito menos
as analoxías topolóxicas explicativas da hipótese)

when she experiences amorous ecstasy, the violence of rapture
—a constitutive violence vague as a snow squall, a swarm of
bees or pale light of a torch inundating gods, omens and
tombs—, thus pleasure—a remote cave, a dark fog, blue,
ashen, grey as a Himalaya—she incises letters in the weft of
papyrus

that grotto, that gloom and the sighs of pleasure articulate the
power of what bursts free in language

Like the dough we roll out till it fills a complete geometry, like a
heap of buds

bodies have consistency, they establish meaning.

What i'm trying to clarify is that, despite its seminal configura-
tion, the authorial court can neither coincide with nor lean
toward either of two counterposed series. All in all, given that
the poem only inscribes itself where its concretion is impossible
(outside the archive or the already-recorded), it can't be faithful to
any of the three described categories. Perhaps this is why insects,
birds and certain mythological creatures (victories, cupids and
she who is messenger of the gods, along with the angelic hierar-
chies) are winged.

Even though the prior bit privileged the simile "a column of
butterflies," the grand canyon dividing the banks of the Sil
could also work, as could the scales of Osiris

(these three comparisons don't exhaust in the least the topolog-
ical analogies that serve to illustrate the hypothesis)

**Tres liñas de presentación en rexistro coloquial para Cracovia

Podería ser así: dunha beira unha imposibilidade de escritura, doutra unha potencia de escritura (son simétricas como as ás dunha bolboreta), no medio Eu: Eu é unha greta. O poema inventa o que non concorda, só é leal á súa propia independencia e fermosura.

**Three lines of introduction in a colloquial register, for Krakow

Look at it this way: over here, the impossibility of writing, over there, a power of writing (symmetrical like butterfly wings),in the middle, *I: I* is a fissure. The poem invents that which doesn't reconcile, is only loyal to its own independence and beauty.

Agora ben: as glándulas propiamente non falan; cando son inducidas a unha secreción veloz, en situacións de clausura, despoboamento ou tránsito, xeran no alento unha invasión mínima; o mesmo que un amante ou mirada imaxinaria proxectan un alude—celeste—de arquitectura-osíxeno global na carne

chamarémoslle a esta disfunción *desdobre irreal* ou *alucinación hipofisíaca*

cando estes mensaxeiros dominan a imaxinación a razón desertízase (un ermo calquera no que quizais e en estado non doméstico pasten camelos): son os diálogos da hipófise

e gustaríalle, gustaríalle, pero moito, que a disolución dos seus órganos encarnase letras sobre os solos pardos e occidentais, o mesmo que os demais animais, ata que formasen un amplo sepulcro, nunha das últimas *fronteiras terrestres*. E os perigos da súa arte sen fundamento, orientada como os liques cara a unha quimérica escritura dos estros, cara ao norte (todo iso que le nos libros, que lle sucede)

verdadeiramente o que ten é un cofre de dor

e ningún escándalo lle causa a ausencia de significado na raíz

desta maneira e perdidos xa todos os acordos debería facerme o solsticio —a min—esvelta.

Okay now: glands don't speak; when induced to rapid secretion, in times of closure, depopulation or movement, they only minimally invade the breath: just like a lover or imaginary gaze projects an avalanche—heavenly—of global architectural-oxygen upon the flesh

let's call this dysfunction *unreal deployment* or *pituitarial hallucination*

when these messengers take over the imagination, reason desertifies (any vacant field where camels perhaps graze undomesticated): it's the pituitary talking

and she wanted, wanted badly, that the dissolution of her organs incarnate letters on dark western soils, just like other animals do, until they form a huge tomb, at one of the farthest *earthly frontiers*. And the perils of her unfounded art, pointed like lichen toward a chimaerical writing of estrus, toward north (everything she reads in books, it happens to her)

really what she has is a vault of pain

and no scandal brings her the absence of root significance

in this way and with all deals already foundered, i'll have to make the solstice —my solstice—svelte.

GORAN SIMIC
TRANSLATES *STEVAN TONTIĆ* (Serbo-Croatian)

A Short History of the Poet's Life

Recently I took the trip back to Bosnia-Herzegovina, the country where I was born, to meet the ghosts of the past who haunt me every time I return, no matter how loudly I say how happy I am to live in Canada. I don't need to explain my feelings to the people who happen to belong to the same tribe, those who crossed the border to a new life with one leg in the future and the other in the past. They know the strange pain of balancing past and present that no doctor can heal.

There I met Stevan Tontić (b.1946), who, prior to war, was one of most revered poets in Sarajevo, in Bosnia-Herzegovina, and in Yugoslavia. Sarajevo has slowly moved from being a multicultural city to a multi-Muslim city. But this is an issue to discuss some other time, when we humans reach the point at which we agree that politics should be separated from religion, again.

As a young poet about 35 years ago, looking for revolution to occur first in the field of poetry instead of politics, I belonged to the generation of urban poets and Stevan belonged to the poets who emerged after World War Two. There were poetical differences between us. Though my younger generation respected the writing of Stevan's group, and adored the same world poets, we gently fought him, using jokes, irony, and drinking sessions. It took us time to understand that writing is not a horse race.

Now that Stevan Tontić and I realize that the gap between our generations shrank the moment we noticed we were all grey-haired, there are two major reasons for me to translate him: 1. He remains one of the greatest poets in the Balkans. 2. The phases in his life remind me of my own.

In 1992, I met Stevan in besieged Sarajevo to present him with two onions, at a time when food was the official currency on the black market. In 1995, I met him in Berlin, where he was serving the sentence of a refugee, and he bought me a pasta meal in a restaurant where the waiter didn't even try to hide how tired he was of cheap customers. Most recently, we read at the Sarajevo poetry festival. We had fun remembering how different we were before we got grey hair. Stevan lives in Sarajevo now. I live in Toronto.

These three poems, which I translated with the usual help from my friend, the poet Fraser Sutherland, who has met Stevan Tontić, reflect three phases in a poet's life. In each poem that sounds sometimes as a prayer, one can read the drama of the poet who happens to witness a world that changed for worse. Between the lines there is layer of pain in which I recognize myself.

Kuća u nebu

Naša kuća na brežuljku
Bila se orodila s nebom
Svaka hulja od anđela mogla je da nas
Kibicuje
Svaki ološ odozgo
Znao je
Imamo li soli za večeru !

Kuća se toliko slizala s nebom
Kćeri nebeske kradom su prljale
Usne na tijelima nas braće
Bilo je trenutaka—bogu je od naše familije
Mrak na oči padao.

Nebo se svijalo oko našeg gnijezda
Kao oko raja
Braća su likovala
Gunđao tata
Suzila majka.

Dara je prevršila mjeru
Zapržiću im čorbu !-reče otac
Pa opali uvis iz proste
Lovačke puške.

Nasta takav mir
Hoćeš-nećeš mogao si čuti kako postojiš
A gore se svako- nego šta-
Posvetio poslu za koji je plaćen !

The House in the Sky

Our house atop the hill
Got so close to the sky
Every scoundrel angel could observe us
And the rabble up above
Could tell if we put salt on the table.

Our house became so chummy with the sky
Celestial daughters secretly soiled their lips
On the bodies of my brothers and me.
Sometimes God was driven out of His mind
Because of our family.

The sky curled around our nest
As if around paradise.
We brothers rejoiced.
Father grumbled.
Mother wept.

That was the last straw.
"This is enough!" father said
And fired a round from his hunting rifle
Straight into the sky.

It became so quiet
You could hear you existed
Whether you liked it or not.
And above—what else?
Everybody did what he was paid to do.

Granica

Ne mičući s kućnog praga,
ne odmičući se ni za lakat od ženina skuta,
probudih se u novoj državi,
kaže mi znanac.

Granica je povučena
posred srca.

Razum je počeo da shvata i právda,
ludo srce lupa i poriče.

Ja se teturam:
ni uspravljen, nov korak da bacim,
ni oboren, u zemlju da legnem.

Border

Without moving across the threshold
Without straying an inch from my wife's apron
I woke up in a new country,
So my friend told me.

The border was drawn
Straight through my heart.

The intellect starts to understand and justify,
But the crazy thumping heart repudiates.

I'm still staggering,
Neither upright, to take a new step,
Nor thrown on my back, to lie in the dirt.

Hvala ti, smrti

Hvala ti, smrti:
Jedino mi ti daješ snagu
da podnesem ovu provalu čudâ
u moj "život".
Jedino ti, majčice.

Duša je moja čvrsta,
jasna i odlučna,
mišice mi trunu.

Da nije tebe,
u šta bih se, mila moja,
ja dosad prometnuo?

Ovako sam spokojan,
konačno sabran,
sam sa sobom kao pred licem Božjim,
zatvoren u skafander svog tijela
koje već odlažem od sebe,
ja—sin tvoj, smrti,
ja koji te tražim od časa samog rođenja,
predavši se snu o nepostojanju.

Thank You, Death

Thank you, death,
Only from you I gain the strength
To bear this outbreak of miracles
In my so-called life,
Only from you, my little mother.

My soul is solid,
Clear, and decisive,
My muscles are numb.

Without you
My dear one,
What would I have become?

I am at least serene,
Calm at last,
At one with myself as before the face of God,
Locked in the spacesuit of my body
Which I am already tearing off.

I, death, who am your son,
Who searched for you since I was born
Surrender to not being me, or anyone.

PRISCILA UPPAL
TRANSLATES *JOÃO DA CRUZ E SOUSA* (Portuguese)
(with assistance in the Portuguese by Vivian Ralickas)

Who could resist translating work from a poet who has a book called *Ultimos sonetos* (Ultimate Sonnets)? Add to the weightiness of such a title a personal history of oppression and triumph (a nineteenth-century Black man, born to slave parents in Brazil, he diligently pursued his literary ambitions despite poverty and blatant racism to become one of the most beloved and cosmopolitan of Brazilian poets) and a dearth of English translations of this brave and fascinating man's work, I jumped at the opportunity to work with my friend Dr. Vivian Ralickas and delve into João da Cruz e Sousa's poetic sensibility and to find an equivalent voice for the witty, angry, political, sensual, even obscene lines of this Brazilian Baudelaire in modern English.

Our translating sessions were fun, heady, inspiring, invigorating. We started over email, Vivian sending me the original Portuguese sonnets, which she had colour-coded with computer highlighting to indicate end and internal rhymes, alongside very literal English transcriptions of the poems, appended with footnotes explaining nuances, references, possible double and triple meanings. I then worked on English poetic versions of the poems for many weeks, balancing the connotations of English words alongside the Portuguese, debating how to abandon the rhyme scheme – which would sound too heavy-handed in English – but maintain the beauty of the music of the original, examining line after line for consistency of voice and vision, even reading the incomprehensible (to me) Portuguese over and over out loud to get an instinctive, guttural feel for the rhythms and emotional transitions and resonances of the language.

Once I was relatively pleased with the results, I sent these versions to her; she sent me more detailed notes on each line or sometimes even a word. I reworked the poems again, resent them, and later on we met for several hours to discuss, debate, and even torture out choicer phrases to decide on the final versions included here.

Brazilians are dramatic, hyperbolic, in ways that are natural to their culture and their language, and so I wanted to find ways to match that drama in the sexual or racial tensions in Cruz e Sousa's poems. Eventually our discussions rested on the question: how to express the voice of a man who was more hated the more famous he became? The sonnet, his dominant poetic form of choice, allowed for controlled rage, as well as wonderful exhibition of his technical poetic abilities in mastering this European tradition. I wanted to render that rage, mixed with sophistication and elegance, in English, as it is in Portuguese. Occasionally, this meant taking a few liberties with actual imagery – translated literally some of it would be completely opaque and seem silly to an English reader – especially in the last poem, which I have translated as "Dethroned Beauty," though the title is literally "Dead Beauty." But "dead beauty" didn't give the sense of adoration and admiration in the speaker's voice to my mind. Dethroned beauty implied that she once held a high, imperial position over the admirer, something the rest of the poem's imagery confirmed. The final lines of the poem also required deviation from the original on my part, so that the poem's music becomes concise, and decisive, while maintaining a sad nostalgia for what once was and how people hold on to such youthful memories. A literal translation would be: "As though still the final draughts/Of opulence, of pomp and luxury,/The healthy relics of beauty." My version ends: "The final hangovers of opulence,/of splendour and luxury:/ the souvenirs of beauty," also an apt description of how I felt after translating these works.

Escravocratas

Oh! Trânsfugas do bem que sob o manto régio
Manhosos, agachados—bem como um crocodilo,
Viveis sensualmente à *luz* dum privilégio
Na *pose* bestial dum cágado tranqüilo

Eu rio-me de vós e cravo-vos as setas
Ardentes do olhar—formando uma vergasta
Dos raios mil do sol, das iras dos poetas,
E vibro-vos à espinha—enquanto o grande basta

O basta gigantesco, imenso, extraordinário—
Da branca consciência—o rútilo sacrário
No tímpano do ouvido—audaz me não soar.

Eu quero em rude verso altivo adamastórioco,
Vermelho, colossal, d'estrépito, gongórico,
Castrar-vos como um touro—ouvindo-vos urrar!

Slave Masters

Damn you, Deserters of Good, on your royal perches,
crouched and cunning—like a crocodile,
living the high life, basking in the limelight of privilege,
cleverly posing as peaceful animals.

I laugh in your face and stab you with the switchblades
of my eyes—flogging your back
with the sun's endless rays, with the disdain of the poets
warping your spine—while the great *end*,

the gigantic *over*, immense, extraordinary—
of the white conscience, the red reliquary
in the inner ear—dares me to hold my tongue.

I want—in rude, arrogant, revolutionary style,
in colossal, powerful, earth-shattering red!—
To castrate you like a bull—Hear you howl!

Acrobata da dor

Gargalha, ri, num riso de tormenta,
Como um palhaço, que desengonçado,
Nervoso, ri, num riso absurdo, inflado
De uma ironia e de uma dor violenta.

Da gargalhada atroz, sanguinolenta,
Agita os guizos, e convulsionado
Salta, gavroche, salta clown, varado
Pelo estertor dessa agonia lenta...

Pedem-te bis e um bis não se despreza!
Vamos! reteza os músculos, reteza
Nessas macabras piruetas d'aço...

E embora caias sobre o chão, fremente,
Afogado em teu sangue estuoso e quente
Ri! Coração, tristíssimo palhaço.

The Acrobat of Pain

Cackle! Cry! Like a clown
in tormented laughter, who, contorted,
anxious, laughs, an absurd laugh, overblown
with irony and violent sounds.

With atrocious, bloody laughter
ring your bells—convulse—
Jump—low-life! Jump clown! Beaten
down by the monotony of agony...

Encore! Encore! Encores are not to be scoffed at!
Move it! Harden your muscles, harden them
into macabre steel pirouettes...

Inevitably falling to the floor, shaking
drowned in your hot, boiled blood.
Laugh! The heart is the saddest clown.

Alucinação

Ó solidão do Mar, ó amargor das vagas,
Ondas em convulsões, ondas em rebeldia,
Desespero do Mar, furiosa ventania,
Boca em fel dos tritões engasgada de pragas.

Velhas chagas do sol, ensangüentadas chagas
De ocasos purpurais de atroz melancolia,
Luas tristes, fatais, da atra mudez sombria
Da trágica ruína em vastidões pressagas.

Para onde tudo vai, para onde tudo voa,
Sumido, confundido, esboroado, à-toa,
No caos tremendo e nu dos tempos a rolar?

Que Nirvana genial há de engolir tudo isto—
—Mundos de Inferno e Céu, de Judas e de Cristo,
Luas, chagas do sol e turbilhões do Mar?!

Hallucination

Oh solitude of the sea, oh bitterness of the waves,
waves in convulsions, waves in rebellions,
deep despair of the sea, furious winds,
mouth stabbed by Tritons, suffocated by plagues.

Scorched wounds of the earth, bloody wounds,
with its purple sunsets of endless suffering,
its sad fatal moons darkening, mute
on the vast tragic ruin to come.

Where does everything go? Where does everything fly?
Vanished, useless, undone, destroyed
in the vast naked chaos of the future?

What ingenious Nirvana will have to swallow all of this—
worlds of Heaven and Hell, Judas and Christ,
moons, the earth's wounds, the maelstroms of the sea?

Lubricidade

Quisera ser a serpe venenosas
Que dá-te medo e dá-te pesadelos
Para envolver-me, ó Flor maravilhosa,
Nos flavos turbilhões dos teus cabelos.

Quisera ser a serpe veludosa
Para, enroscada em múltiplos novelos,
Saltar-te aos seios de fluidez cheirosa
E babujá-los e depois mordê-los...

Talvez que o sangue impuro e flamejante
Do teu lânguido corpo de bacante,
De langue ondulação de águas do Reno

Estranhamente se purificasse...
Pois que um veneno de áspide vorace
Deve ser morto com igual veneno...

Lasciviousness

I wanted to be the poisonous snake
filling you with fear and spawning nightmares,
tangling myself, oh intoxicating flower,
in the golden pit of your hair.

I wanted to be the velvet snake,
who, coiled like a simple ball of yarn,
pounces at your bountiful breasts,
slobbering on them, and then bites...

Maybe it's that your glorious, impure blood,
flowing through your goddess' body
like the languid undulations of the Rhine

strangely purified itself...
Just as the lethal poison of an asp
must be murdered with equal venom...

Monja

Ó Lua, Lua triste, amargurada,
Fantasma de brancuras vaporosas,
A tua nívea luz ciliciada
Faz murchecer e congelar as rosas.

Nas floridas searas ondulosas,
Cuja folhagem brilha fosforeada,
Passam sombras angélicas, nivosas,
Lua, Monja da cela constelada.

Filtros dormentes dão aos lagos quietos,
Ao mar, ao campo, os sonhos mais secretos,
Que vão pelo ar, noctâmbulos, pairando...

Então, ó Monja branca dos espaços,
Parece que abre para mim os braços,
Fria, de joelhos, trêmula, rezando...

The Nun

Oh Moon, Sad Moon, embittered,
pale, white, anemic ghost,
your cold, penitent light
wilts and freezes all the roses.

In the lush, sweeping fields,
where flowers shine like phosphorous,
your angelic shadows fall like snowflakes,
Moon, Oh Nun of the constellations.

Your veil of sleep gives to the quiet lakes,
to the sea, to the fields, the most secret dreams
afloat on the air, noctambulists, hovering...

Then, Oh White Nun of the sky,
is it possible you open your arms to me;
So cold, on your knees, trembling, praying...

Beleza morta

De leve, louro e enlanguescido helianto
Tens a flórea dolência contristada...
Há no teu riso amargo um certo encanto
De antiga formosura destronada.

No corpo, de um letárgico quebranto,
Corpo de essência fina, delicada,
Sente-se ainda o harmonioso canto
Da carne virginal, clara e rosada.

Sente-se o canto errante, as harmonias
Quase apagadas, vagas, fugidias
E uns restos de clarão de Estrela acesa...

Como que ainda os derradeiros haustos
De opulências, de pompas e de faustos,
As relíquias saudosas da beleza.

Dethroned Beauty

My light, blonde, languished sunflower,
you have a growing, grieving melancholy...
There is in your bitter laugh a certain charm
of an old dethroned beauty.

On your body, lethargic, exhausted, weak,
can still be felt the harmonious song,
the delicate, fine essence
of virginal flesh, smooth and flush.

But also the wandering song, the harmony
almost extinguished, fading ephemerally
and the dusty light of a once brilliant star...

The final hangovers of opulence,
of slendour and luxury:
the souvenirs of beauty.

PAUL VERMEERSCH
TRANSLATES HERMAN DE CONINCK (Dutch)

When I was asked to contribute to this anthology of transla-
tions, I knew right away that I wanted to translate the work
of the Belgian poet Herman de Coninck. I had two main rea-
sons for this. First, it gave me a chance to engage with a part
of my own Flemish heritage head-on. Indeed, in my life I have
had very little exposure to Belgian literature in general and
Flemish poetry in particular. As J.M. Coetzee pointed out in his
book of translations of Dutch-language poems *Landscape with
Rowers: Poetry from the Netherlands*, "Dutch is a minor lan-
guage in the sense that it is spoken by only some fifteen mil-
lion people, and its literature is a minor literature in the
sense that it is not widely read." It is not minor, however, in
its artistic accomplishments. And that brings me to my sec-
ond reason for choosing Herman de Coninck. I was already
somewhat familiar with, and certainly impressed by, his warm,
surprising and magnanimous poetry. He is not only one of
the most widely read of modern Belgian poets, but he is one
of the most widely read poets in the Dutch language of all
time. Despite his enormous popularity in Europe, only one
volume of translations of his poems into English exists: *The
Plural of Happiness: Selected Poems of Herman De Coninck*
translated by Laure-Anne Bosselaar and Kurt Brown (Oberlin
College Press, 2006). Since I've been an admirer of de Coninck's
poetry since I first read one of his poems in translation many
years ago, I couldn't ignore this opportunity to share some of
his work with a new Canadian audience. There was one hur-
dle, however, that had to be surmounted before this could
happen – I barely speak a word of Dutch. I am indebted to a
handful of people who prepared literal translations for me to

work from, as well as footnotes on connotations, subtexts and allusions that would be, quite literally, foreign to me. In particular, I would like thank Kathryn Kuitenbrouwer for her invaluable assistance on two of the poems included here. It has been a genuine pleasure easing these Dutch-language poems into their new English versions. I hope the readers of this adventurous book derive similar pleasure from reading them.

"Hij had gehoopt dat het zonder herfst kon"

Hij had gehoopt dat het zonder herfst kon.
Ineens sneeuw. De ascese van wit. De precisie van kou.
Minder moet zorgen voor betekenis,
meer moet ervan genezen—

en dat het dan gedaan was. Niet dit maanden-
lange afhaken van laatste blaren, uitsorteren
van rommel, zó eindeloos uitpakken met gemis
dat je de blaren terug zou hangen aan hun takken.

Hij had gehoopt dat het zonder verzuren kon.
Maar de hele tuin ligt te gisten van uren
tegen, en bijna te sissen van één minuut zon.
O, toen alles nog voorbij kon gaan en niets hoefde te duren.

"He had hoped there didn't have to be an autumn"

He had hoped there didn't have to be an autumn.
Only sudden snow. The asceticism of white. The precision of cold.
With no need for all the usual symbolism,
people could just be cured of it,

and then it would just be over. Not all these months
of falling leaves, like sorting through
garbage, unpacking such an endless sense of loss
you feel you have to hang each leaf back on its branch.

He had hoped there didn't have to be this acidic rot.
But now the whole garden is fermenting from the hours
of rain, and then it practically sizzles in a moment of sunlight.
Oh, for the days when things could end without having to last forever.

Ballade van de traagheid

Ik hou van de traagheid van liggen in het gras, als een vorst:
ik, uitkijkend over mijn aanhangers,
mijn ledematen, zeggend tot mijn linkerarm:
jij daar, breng mijn hand eens voor
mijn mond, dat ik geeuw, in orde,
ga maar weer liggen, goed zo,
tucht moet ik hier hebben.

Ik hou van de traagheid van zijn,
zen, zegt men in het oosten, ik geloof dat het
hetzelfde is.
Ik hou van de traagheid van liggen in bed,
Jij naast mij, je knie in mijn knie-
holtes, als twee s'en, de traagheid waarmee je me
niet gezegd hebt dat je al wakker was,
je uit lippen bestaande ontvankelijkheid,
de traagheid waarmee ik sneller en sneller kom,
de kalmte waarmee ik wilder en wilder word,
de traagheid van jouw diplomatisch lichaam
dat geeft en neemt, jouw corps diplomatique,

en de traagheid van een sigaar nadien,
de traagheid van grandeur, de traagheid van wie
zich te pletter rijdt tegen een boom in vertraagde
film, het majestuose van een ontploffing, plechtig,
plechtig eindigt dit leven.

The Ballad of Slowness

I love the slowness of lying on the grass like a king:
there I am, surveying all my subjects,
my limbs, saying to my left arm:
you there, bring my hand to my mouth
that I might yawn, yes,
and now lie down again, very good,
I demand such discipline.

I love the slowness of *is*,
or Zen, as they say in the East,
it's all the same to me.
I love the slowness of lying in bed,
with you next to me, your knees behind
my knees, spooning, and the slowness with which
you wait to tell me that you're awake,
your movements beginning only in your lips,
the slowness with which I come faster and faster,
the calmness with which I grow wilder and wilder,
the slowness of your diplomatic body
that gives and takes, your *corps diplomatique*,

and the slowness of a cigar afterwards,
the slowness of this grandeur, the slowness of a man
crashing his car into a tree in slow
motion, the majesty of the explosion, solemnly,
solemnly ending this life.

"Meisje op straat laat ballon los"

Meisje op straat laat ballon los.
Geef ook mij maar van die wanhoop,
van die hemelhoge kleine. En wil jij
dan ook zo uit het gezicht verdwijnen?

Ik heb jou toch ook maar per ongeluk
losgelaten? Tot waar ik niet meer kon komen?
Laat mij achterblijven. Heb mij niet meegenomen.

"A girl loses her balloon in the street."

A girl loses her balloon in the street.
Give me some of that despair, too,
from that high little heaven. And isn't that
the way you disappeared from view, as well?

Didn't I accidentally let go
of you? And then how could I follow?
Leave me behind. Don't take me with you.

1958

1.

Mijn oom is dood. Ik mag naar zijn begravenis
met mijn moeder. Ik ben zelden zo van haar geweest.
Daarna koffiekoeken, begravenisfeest, de groot honger
van verdriet. Hoe't met mijn vader is. Hij is er niet.

Ook thuis niet. En mijn moeders zwijgen
duurt voor de dood van slechts een broer te lang.
En de pastoor komt te dikwijls op visite.
Blijkt: mijn vader is bij de politie moeten blijven

omdat zijn boekhouding niet in ordee was.
Daar is hij ziek geworden van niet bij ons te kunnen zijn.
En nu moest hij daar blijven tot hij weer genezen was.

Daar: dat bleek Merkplas.
Anders jongens gaan met hun vader vissen.
Ik heb een vader die ziek is van mij te moeten missen.

2.

Pas jaren later, ik ben twintig, ma ik weten,
ik moest begrijpen dat't hem moeilijk viel,
mouja, dat hij niet homosexsueel was,
of toch maar een klein beetje: pedofiel.

En dat hij daarom toen gevangen had gezeten.
Ik ben vier. Ik mag bij hem op de canapé.
Ik moet doen of ik slaap. Hij doet mee.
Ineens ben ik honderdduizend haartjes.

1958

1.

My uncle is dead. I should go to his funeral
with my mother. I've rarely been so close to her.
Then there's coffee cakes, a funeral buffet, the huge appetite
of grief. And what about my father? He's not here.

He's not at home, either. So my mother's silence
lasts too long to mourn for a single brother.
Maybe the priest visits too often.
In fact, my father is still in police custody

because his accounting is a little sketchy.
He got sick there because he misses us so much.
And now he has to stay until he's better.

Well, that's Merksplas* for you.
The other boys go fishing with their fathers.
And my father is sick from missing me.

2.

So a few years later, I am twenty, I know some things,
and I finally understand how difficult it was for him.
Okay, so he wasn't a homosexual,
but maybe just a bit of a pedophile.

And that's why he sat in prison.
I am four years old. My father and I are on the couch.
I have to pretend I'm sleeping. So does he.
Suddenly, I am one hundred thousand tiny hairs.

---

*Merksplas is a town in Belgium known for its jail.

Huivelingwekkend is het, mezelf te zijn.
Als het voorbij is voel ik nog lang hoe recht
ze hebben gestaan, één voor één, hoevele.

Pas nu denk ik: hij kietelde mij,
uren, niet om me te doen lachen,
maar omdat hij niet durfde te strelen.

It's a ghastly, ghastly thing, being me.
When it's over I can feel how long, how straight
they stood on end, one by one, and how many.

It occurs to me now: he tickled me,
for hours, not to make me laugh,
but because he didn't dare caress me.

"Mijn vriend imiteert ongeveer alles"

Mijn vriend imiteert ongeveer alles.
Gisteren nog oefende hij het wateren
van een verslenst bureaucraatje in:
het klonk als heel zijn leven,
een stille sisser.
En vandaag sit ie te eten,
steekt een sigaar op, bestelt twee rode wijn
en declameert: de wroeging van Nixon.
En plots loopt hij hard weg en verbergt zich
achter een hoek. Wat doe je nou,
vraag ik. Ik ben geluk roept hij,
je vindt me nooit.

En's avonds verandert de sfeer,
altijd. Velden rusten als brede bedden
en de nevel legt overal spreien.
Slapen is iets wat ik tegenwoordig
nog enkel kan imiteren, zegt hij.
Liefde ook, zeg ik. We zwijgen.
En later bootst hij het geluid na
van een autootje on mee naar
de maan to rijden.

"My friend imitates more-or-less everything."

My friend imitates more-or-less everything.
Just yesterday he practiced pissing like
a failed little bureaucrat:
it sounded just like the rest of his life,
a slow hiss.
And today he sits down to eat,
lights up a cigar, orders two red wines
and declares: the repentance of Nixon.
Then all of a sudden he runs away and hides
behind a corner. What are you doing now?
I ask. I am happiness, he answers,
you'll never find me.

And in the evening the atmosphere changes,
always. Fields stretch out like wide beds,
and a mist is spread over everything.
Nowadays, sleep is something
that I can only imitate, he says.
Love, too, I say. And we are silent.
Later on, he will imitate the sound
made by a car designed
for driving to the moon.

DARREN WERSHLER
TRANSLATES *EZRA POUND* (English into QR Code)

The Pound Matrices

Poetry is the art of making communication more complex by attempting to simplify it.

In 1919, Ezra Pound edited and published Ernest Fenollosa's essay "The Chinese Written Character as a Medium for Poetry." Fenollosa argued, infamously, that, unlike the arbitrary relationship between the letters of the Roman alphabet and the sounds they represent, Chinese ideograms are, to some extent, direct images of the things that they signify. Regardless of the veracity of Fenollosa's claim (scholars have been debating it ever since), it became Pound's inspiration for the poetics of early Imagism. "In a Station of the Metro" is the epitome of the ideogrammatic method, juxtaposing two disparate images ("these faces in the crowd" and "petals on a wet, black bough") to produce a new matrix of meaning.

In a contemporary context, both the abstract form of this image – a variegated field of black and white pixels – and the notion of a poem as a kind of ideogrammatic matrix immediately invoke comparison with two-dimensional barcodes. Pound was fascinated with the formal aesthetics of machinery, and, later in his career, came to argue for a "machine art" where there would be a direct correspondence between beauty and use-value. Accordingly, I have translated a number of Pound's short Imagist poems (or particularly relevant fragments from these poems) into QR ("Quick Response") Codes. There are many subspecies of two-dimensional barcodes, but QR Codes, created by the Japanese company Denso-Wave in 1994, are the most popular ones in use in Asia at the moment. Turnabout is fair play.

I've chosen to describe these pieces as translations rather than encodings because, as in any translation process, making and reading a QR Code doesn't produce fully symmetrical texts; retranslating the QR Code to English will result in something that differs slightly from the source. Some QR code readers, for example, render all text as centre-justified, which has the potential to substantially alter the appearance (and interpretation) of a given poem. Many existing QR encoders have an upper limit of 250 characters, so I have only encoded key portions of the longer poems in this section (which ones? You'll have to decode them for yourself to find out).

These translations also serve as a commentary on the politics and economics that informed Pound's fascism and anti-semitism. Given his paranoia about differentiating between linguistic exchange and financial exchange, it is especially satisfying to point out that the two are never far apart; as bpNichol pointed out many years after Pound with his 'Pataphysical Hardware Company, "all that signifies can be sold." The conclusion of Pound's "A Pact" makes a grudging proposition to Walt Whitman: "let there be commerce between us"; translating the poem into a barcode seals the deal.

◆

A note on reading these poems: they are meant for mechanical eyes, but software is available for many camera-equipped cell phones that will do the translation work for you. On the iPhone, for example, as of this writing, a number of options exist: BeeTagg reader, 2D Sense and UpCode (all of which are free), and QR Reader (which is available for a nominal fee). Of these options, the one that seems most reliable is BeeTagg.

In a Station of the Metro

The apparition of these faces in the crowd;
Petals on a wet, black bough.

A Pact

I make a pact with you, Walt Whitman—
I have detested you long enough.
I come to you as a grown child
Who has had a pig-headed father;
I am old enough now to make friends.
It was you that broke the new wood,
Now is a time for carving.
We have one sap and one root—
Let there be commerce between us.

And the days are not full enough

And the days are not full enough
And the nights are not full enough
And life slips by like a field mouse
　Not shaking the grass.

Fan-Piece, For Her Imperial Lord

O fan of white silk,
clear as frost on the grass-blade,

You also are laid aside.

The Seeing Eye

The small dogs look at the big dogs;
They observe unwieldy dimensions
And curious imperfections of odor.
Here is the formal male group:
The young men look upon their seniors,
They consider the elderly mind
And observe its inexplicable correlations.

Said Tsin-Tsu:
It is only in small dogs and the young
That we find minute observation.

NOTES ON CONTRIBUTORS

Jan-Willem Anker (b. 1978) has had poems published in periodicals such as *Bunker Hill*, *Awater*, *DWB*, *Kinbote* and *Poëziekrant*. For his debut collection *Inzinkingen* (2005), he was awarded the Jo Peters Poëzieprijs. *Donkere arena* ("Dark Arena") and *Luchthaven* ("Airport") both appeared in 2006. He lives in Amsterdam.

Oana Avasilichioaei (b. 1977) has published *feria: a poempark* (Wolsak & Wynn, 2008), *Abandon* (Wolsak & Wynn, 2005) and a translation of Nichita Stănescu, *Occupational Sickness* (BuschekBooks, 2006). A collaborative work with Erín Moure, *Expeditions of a Chimæra*, is upcoming fall 2009 (BookThug).

Ken Babstock (b. 1970) was born in Newfoundland and now lives in Toronto, where he works as an editor, freelance writer, and teacher. He is the author of *Mean* (1999) which won the Milton Acorn Award and the Atlantic Poetry Prize, *Days into Flatspin* (2001), and *Airstream Land Yacht* (2006) which was a finalist for the Governor General's Award, the Winterset Prize, the Griffin Prize, and won Ontario's Trillium Prize for Poetry. His poems have been translated into German, Dutch, Serbo-Croatian, Czech, and French.

Christian Bök (b. 1966) is the author not only of *Crystallography* (Coach House Press, 1994), a 'pataphysical encyclopedia nominated for the Gerald Lampert Memorial Award, but also of *Eunoia* (Coach House Books, 2001), a bestselling work of experimental literature, which has gone on to win the Griffin Poetry Prize. Bök has created artificial languages for two television shows: Gene Roddenberry's *Earth: Final Conflict* and Peter Benchley's *Amazon*. Bök has also earned many accolades for his virtuoso performances of sound poetry (particularly the

Ursonate by Kurt Schwitters). His conceptual artworks (which include books built out of Rubik's cubes and Lego bricks) have appeared at the Marianne Boesky Gallery in New York City as part of the exhibit *Poetry Plastique*. Bök is currently a professor of English at the University of Calgary.

Dionne Brand (b. 1953) is a poet, novelist and essayist living in Toronto. Her nine volumes of poetry include *No Language Is Neutral*, nominated for the Governor General's Award, *Land to Light On* which won the Governor General's Award and the Trillium Award for Literature in 1997. Brand's *thirsty* was nominated for the Trillium Prize for Literature, the Griffin Poetry Prize and the Toronto Book Award in 2003. It won the Pat Lowther Award. Her 2006 volume of poetry, *Inventory,* was nominated for the Governor General's Award, the Pat Lowther Award and the Trillium Prize for Literature. Her last novel *What We All Long For* won the 2006 Toronto Book Award. Other fiction includes the novel *In Another Place Not Here* – a 1998 *New York Times* Notable Book and *At the Full and Change of the Moon* a *Los Angeles Times* Notable Book of the Year, 1999. Works of non-fiction include *Bread Out of Stone* and *A Map to the Door of No Return*. She is Professor of English in the School of English and Theatre Studies, University of Guelph.

Nicole Brossard (b. 1943). Poet, novelist and essayist, twice Governor General's Award winner for her poetry, Nicole Brossard has published more than thirty books since 1965 and has won numerous national and international awards. Many among those books have been translated into English: *Mauve Desert, The Aerial Letter, Picture Theory, Lovhers, Baroque at Dawn, The Blue Books, Installations, Museum of Bone and Water* and more recently *Intimate Journal, Fluid Arguments, Yesterday at the Hotel Clarendon* and *Notebook of roses and civilization*. Her work has also been widely translated into English, Spanish, German,

Italian, Norwegian, Japanese, Slovenian, Romanian, Catalan and others languages. Nicole Brossard writes and lives in Mont-réal.

Barry Callaghan (b. 1937) is an award-winning poet, novelist, publisher and journalist. His works include *Hogg: The Poems and Drawings*, *The Black Queen Stories*, *When Things Get Worst*, *A Kiss Is Still a Kiss*, and the memoir *Barrelhouse Kings*. His writing has been published around the world and translated into many languages. He is considered one of Canada's great men of letters, and has won the W.O. Mitchell Award for a body of work, the CBC Fiction Prize, the foundation of the Advancement of Canadian Letters Prize for Fiction, among others. His latest works are *Between Trains*, a book of short stories, and *Beside Still Waters*, a novel.

George Elliott Clarke (b. 1960). Born in Windsor, Nova Scotia, a seventh-generation Africadian, of mixed Aboriginal and African (Negro) heritage. Principally a poet, his acclaimed works include the verse-novel *Whylah Falls* (1990), the play and opera *Beatrice Chancy* (1999), the narrative lyric suite *Execution Poems* (2000), the scholarly essays *Odysseys Home: Mapping African-Canadian Literature* (2002), and the novel *George & Rue* (2005). His honours number the Governor General's Award for Poetry (2001), the National Magazine Gold Award for Poetry (2001), the Martin Luther King Jr. Achievement Award (2004), the Pierre Elliott Trudeau Fellowship Prize (2005-08), and the Dartmouth Book Award for Fiction (2006). His latest books are *Blues & Bliss* (2008), selected poems edited by Jon Paul Fiorentino, and *I & I* (2009), a verse-novel. The inaugural E.J. Pratt Professor of Canadian Literature at the University of Toronto, Clarke was appointed to the Order of Nova Scotia in 2006 and to the Order of Canada in 2008.

Herman de Coninck (1944-1997) was, until his untimely death of heart failure at the age of 53, Belgium's leading poet and one of the most popular Dutch-language poets of all time. He was also an influential literary critic, journalist and publisher. The author of many books of poetry, essays and fiction, de Coninck was celebrated for his ability to write about love and loss with tenderness, humour and fanciful originality. His work received numerous national and international awards.

Geoffrey Cook (b. 1963) was born in Nova Scotia and now teaches English at John Abbott College in Montreal. His first book of poems, *Postscript* (Signal Editions: 2004), includes three translations from Rilke, one of which has also appeared in *Jailbreaks: 99 Canadian Sonnets* (Biblioasis, 2008; ed. Zach Wells). Besides working on a second collection of his own poetry, Geoff is currently translating selected poems by Goethe, Heine, Rilke and Brecht for a forthcoming book.

João da Cruz e Sousa (1861-1898) was born in Santa Catarina, Brazil. At the time of his birth, his mother was free (freed by her owners on her marriage) but his father was not, which meant that by legal definition, he was born into slavery. The parents' owners became Cruz e Sousa's patrons, providing him with an education in literature, languages, math and natural sciences. He began to publish poetry in newspapers in 1877, and he founded the literary newspapers *O Colombo* in 1881 and *O Moleque* ('black boy,' from Kimbundu) in 1885. He campaigned vigorously for Abolition, and he was the first to introduce the approach of French Symbolism to Brazilian Poetry, though he achieved very little fame during his lifetime. His works include *Missal, Broqueis* (prose), and *Ultimos sonetos*. He died of tuberculosis at the age of thirty-seven.

María Elena Cruz Varela (b. 1953) was born on a farm in Colon, Cuba. For the most part self-educated, Varela is a prize-winning Cuban poet who won Cuba's National Award for Poetry in 1989. This prize was given to her by the Union of Cuban Writers and Artists, which subsequently expelled her from its ranks in 1991 for her political views. She is the author of several books of poetry, including *Balada de sangre* (*Ballad of the Blood*), *El ángel agotado* (*The Exhausted Angel*), and *Hija de eva* (*Daughter of Eve*). She was imprisoned in Cuba from 1991-1993. After her release, she was awarded the 1993 Poetry International Award from the Rotterdam Poetry Festival, and the Liberty Prize in the United States. She currently lives in Puerto Rico.

Kiki Dimoula (b. 1931) has twice been awarded the Greek State Prize for Poetry and in 2003 became the first woman to occupy the Chair in Poetry at the Athens Academy. She was married to the poet Athos Dimoulas (1921-1985).

Christopher Doda (b. 1971) is a poet, editor and critic living in Toronto. He is the author of two collections of poetry: *Among Ruins* and *Aesthetics Lesson* both published by Mansfield Press. He is an editor at Exile Editions and *Exile: The Literary Quarterly* and is book review editor for *Studio*, an online poetry journal.

Rishma Dunlop (b. 1956) is an award-winning Canadian poet, playwright, essayist, and fiction writer. Her books of poetry include: *White Album* (Inanna Publications 2008), *Metropolis* (Mansfield Press, 2005), *Reading Like a Girl* (Black Moss Press, 2004), and *The Body of My Garden* (Mansfield Press, 2002). Books as editor include: *Art, Literature, and Place: An Ecopoetics Reader* (CJEE Publications, 2008), *White Ink: Poems on*

Mothers and Motherhood (Demeter Press, 2007), and *Red Silk: An Anthology of South Asian Canadian Women Poets* (Mansfield Press, 2004). She has a PhD from the University of British Columbia and is currently a professor of English and Creative Writing at York University, Toronto. She is founding editor of the international poetry journal *Studio*.

George Faludy (1910-2006). For most of his 22 years in Toronto, George Faludy, widely acknowledged as one of Hungary's greatest poets, lived on St. Mary Street directly across from what is today George Faludy Place, dedicated by the city of Toronto in 2006. Faludy was an outspoken critic of fascism, and was already famous for his translations of the poems of François Villon when he was forced into exile from his native Hungary in 1938. On his return after the Second World War, he was imprisoned in the notorious Recsk labour camp, where he sustained himself and his companions by lecturing in the evenings on art, literature, philosophy and history; and, by composing and committing poems to memory. Released in 1953, he again fled Hungary on the failure of the 1956 Hungarian Uprising, one of 37,000 Hungarian refugees who ultimately came to Canada. In 1962, he published the extraordinary autobiography *My Happy Days in Hell*. In Canada, Faludy wrote, lectured and published several books of poetry in translation, and he became a Canadian citizen. With the toppling of the Berlin Wall in 1989, Faludy returned to Hungary, where he lived and wrote for the next seventeen years.

Steven Heighton (b. 1961) is the author of nine books, most recently the novel *Afterlands*. His poetry and fiction have appeared in many magazines and anthologies, including the *London Review of Books, Poetry Revue, Europe, Tin House, Agni, The Independent, The Walrus,* and *Best English Stories*. His work has been widely translated, has received a number of prizes, and has been nominated for the Governor General's Award, the Trillium Award, a Pushcart Prize, and Britain's W.H. Smith Award.

Horace, or Quintus Horatius Flaccus (65-8 BC), was a Roman poet. During his lifetime he served briefly as a military officer, as a functionary in the Roman treasury, and as a writer, producing satires, epodes, epistles, literary criticism, and poems. He was a highly versatile poet, both formally and thematically; his Odes comprise work ranging from personal lyrics to moralistic verse, and from private, occasional poems to public, ceremonial verse. Horace's words survive not only in Classics departments and in translation (David Ferry's *The Odes of Horace* is deservedly respected and widely read), but in common parlance: the phrase *carpe diem* comes from one of his poems, translated here under the title "Noon on Earth!"

Andréa Jarmai (b. 1953), is originally from Budapest, Hungary, and was raised travelling in Europe and Africa. Subsequently, she lived in Montréal, attending university and working for the rehabilitation of injured birds of prey at McGill University's McDonald Raptor Research and Rehabilitation Centre. In 1990, she moved to Japan, where she taught English and was lead vocalist for the otherwise Japanese band *Fooliar* until 1999, when she returned to Toronto. She has worked at the Metro Zoo as a falconer and animal keeper, and taught ESL to immigrants. With her partner, David Newel, she is also the co-publisher and -editor of Fooliar Press. Her first major collection of poems, *Brother to Dragons, Companion to Owls* (Seraphim Editions, 2004), was followed by *Fools* (LyricalMyrical Press, 2008). Andréa has also published four chapbooks of poems and translations, and is currently working on her first novel, *Thalassa.*

Juan Ramón Jiménez (1881-1958) was one of 20th-century Europe's great poets, and he exercised a profound influence on Spanish culture and especially on the new poetry of García Lorca and others. From 1936, he lived in the United States and Puerto Rico, there producing some of his best work. The Nobel Prize was awarded him in 1956.

Evan Jones (b. 1973) was born in Weston, Ontario, and now lives in Manchester, England. His first collection, *Nothing Fell Today But Rain* (Fitzhenry & Whiteside), was a finalist for the Governor General's Award for Poetry in 2003. He is co-editing an anthology of 20th century Canadian poetry to be published by Carcanet in the U.K.

Sonnet L'Abbé (b. 1973) is the author of two collections of poetry, *A Strange Relief* and *Killarnoe*, both published by McClelland & Stewart. L'Abbé is a regular reviewer for the *Globe and Mail* and has taught creative writing at the University of Toronto. She is currently completing her doctorate in English Literature at the University of British Columbia. Her work has been translated into French and Korean.

A. F. Moritz (b. 1947) has published translations of Spanish and French poetry in various journals, and in books devoted to Ludwig Zeller (Chile), Gilberto Meza (Mexico) and Benjamin Péret (France). His most recent book of poems is *The Sentinel* (2008).

Erín Moure (b. 1955), born in Calgary, lives, translates, and writes poetry in Montreal. As well as translating Chus Pato into English, she has worked with Robert Majzels to translate three books of poetry by Nicole Brossard, has translated one book from the Spanish of Chilean poet Andrés Ajens and one from the Portuguese of Fernando Pessoa. Her most recent book of her own is *O Cadoiro* (Anansi, 2007). Many of her books have been finalists for, or have won awards. Upcoming in 2009 are a book of collaborations with Montreal poet Oana Avasilich-ioaei, *Expeditions of a Chimæra*, from Bookthug; a collection of essays, *My Beloved Wager*, from NeWest Press; and her translation of Pato's *m-Talá* from Shearsman. In 2010 her own *O Resplandor* will appear from Anansi.

Pablo Neruda (1904-1973), the great Chilean poet and the Nobel Laureate (1971), is still – some decades after his death – one of the most influential poets in the world. He was important, of course, because his work was so politically engaged, and so he came to popularily in North America during the turmoil of the 1960s. But in Chile he was equally cherished for his sensual and erotic poetry. His most singular work – aside from *The Heights of Macchu Picchu* – was *Cien sonetos de amor (100 Love Sonnets)*, published in 1959. Exile Editions published a newly translated, bilingual version of *100 Love Sonnets* in 2004, and it was re-released as part of the *Exile Classics* series in 2007.

Chus Pato (b. 1955) lives and teaches in Galicia (a nation in Spain with its own language and culture) and writes in the Galician language. *Hordes of Writing* is her eighth book. She is a poet of rupture and reference in Galicia and Spain, and her much acclaimed work has been translated into Polish, Portuguese, Catalan, Spanish, and English, among others. Her *Charenton* (Vigo: Xerais, 2004) appeared in English translation in 2007 from Shearsman Books in Exeter, UK/BuschekBooks in Canada. The English translation of her *m-Talá* (Vigo: Xerais, 2000) will appear in 2009, and *Hordes of Writing* (Xerais, 2008) likely in 2010 from Shearsman/BuschekBooks. Her latest work, *Secesión*, will appear in Galician in 2009 from Galaxia.

Ezra Pound (1885-1972) was an American expatriate poet, critic and intellectual, and one of the major figures of the Modernist movement and aesthetic in the twentieth century. He was largely responsible for promoting Imagism, coined the term Vorticism, and worked with and influenced nearly all of his contemporaries, including T.S. Eliot, H.D. (Hilda Doolittle), W.B. Yeats, James Joyce, and Williams Carlos Williams. He published dozens of books of original poetry, criticism, and translations. "In a Station of the Metro" is one of the world's most frequently published poems, although his masterpiece is widely considered to be his epic *Cantos*.

Alexander Sergeevich Pushkin (1799-1837). Born in Moscow, Alexander Sergeevich Pushkin won recognition for his genius as a youth, publishing his first poem at 15. He was widely acclaimed, celebrated, and vilified (in some quarters) by the time of graduation from the Imperial Lyceum in Tsarskoe Selo (renamed Pushkin in 1937 by the then-Soviet Union). Adapting French Romanticism, Pushkin modernized Russian literature, conjoining vernacular speech in narratives spun in lyric, dramatic, and satiric modes. His Romantic inclinations also drove him to liberal reformist engagement in politics, which, in Czarist Russia, was radical activities that could have seen him executed or imprisoned. Instead, in the 1820s, he was exiled to southern Russia, his travels restricted, his activites watched, and his writings censored or suppressed. Even so, during this period, Pushkin wrote the imperishable drama *Boris Godunov*, the ever-readable verse-novel *Eugene Onegin*, as well as other lyrics, plays, and stories that still define Russia and render the author the nation's greatest poet. Due to court intrigues involving his wife, Pushkin challenged her said lover to a duel and was mortally wounded in the pursuant gunfire.

Rainer Maria Rilke (1875-1926) was born in Prague and died in Switzerland. One of the most celebrated and influential German poets of the twentieth century, Rilke has become increasingly popular among English readers. Best known for his masterpieces *The Duino Elegies* (1923) and *Sonnets to Orpheus* (1923), the translations here are from his *New Poems* (Part I, 1907 and Part II, 1908), where Rilke achieved his first great verses and articulated a mature poetics.

Arthur Rimbaud (1854-1891) was one of the great French poets of the Symbolist Movement. Rimbaud is famous for composing such masterpieces as "The Drunken Boat," "A Season in Hell," and "Illuminations," all written in his youth during a torrid affair with the poet Paul Verlaine. After completing his best work, Rimbaud disavowed writing completely at the age of 21 in order to live out the remainder of his days as a gunrunner in Africa.

Elisa Sampedrín (b. 1955) was born in Betanzos, Galicia and has lived in Santiago, Vigo, Montreal, Edinburgh, Tokyo. Trained as a mathematician, and active in the anti-Franco student movement in Galicia in the 70s, her work in theatre dates from the 80s, when she lived in Quebec. In 2000, she returned to Europe, where her work now ignores the proscenium and mixes translation, text and performance in what she calls "textual interference," which she sees as a theatre. In keeping with this, she declines the usual machinery of individual publication and publishes only amid the texts of others. One such interference was in Erín Moure's book *Little Theatres*. More recently, she interfered in a collaborative work by Erín Moure and Oana Avasilichioaei, *Expeditions of a Chimœra* (Bookthug, 2009). She lives in Bucharest.

Goran Simic (b. 1952). Born in Bosnia, he moved with his family in 1996 to Canada after the siege of Sarajevo. He has published 15 volumes of poetry, prose, and plays for puppet theatre as well as opera librettos. His works have been translated into more than ten languages and his poetry has been included in international anthologies such as *Scanning the Century* (2000). Among his books published in Canada are the poetry collection *Immigrant Blues* and the short story collection *Yesterday's People*. He lives in Toronto.

Leopold Staff (1878-1957) was born in Lwów. He is the author of 17 books of poetry, several plays, and translated into Polish an astounding amount of literature from several languages, including the works of Heraclitus, Epictetus, da Vinci, Michelangelo, La Rochefoucauld, Spinoza, Diderot, Goethe, Nietzsche, d'Annunzio, Strindberg, and Mann. He was awarded honorary doctorates from the universities in both Krakow and Warsaw and received the PEN Club Prize for his translations. He died at Skarżysko-Kamienna.

Nichita Stănescu (1933-1983) is one of Romania's most important modern poets who published 15 books of poetry including *Necuvintele* (*Unwords*, 1969), *Opere imperfecte* (*Imperfect Works*, 1979), and *Noduri şi semne* (*Knots and Signs*, 1982), as well as four anthologies and two essay collections. His work was translated into many European languages and he was nominated for the Nobel Prize for Literature in 1979.

Stevan Tontić (b. 1948) is a Bosnian poet and translator and one of most distinguished poets in Eastern Europe. He has published 15 volumes of poetry, one novel and is the editor of number of poetry anthologies. After the collapse of the former Yugoslavia, when Bosnian war broke out, Tontić was forced to live in Germany where he published numerous poetry books and won awards. After returning to Bosnia, he became one of the most important poetry translators from the German. He now lives in Sarajevo.

Ko Un (b. 1933) is South Korea's most prolific and internationally recognized writer. A former Buddhist monk and activist, he is author of over 135 books of poetry, fiction, essays and drama. Considered one of Korea's "living myths" for his breathtaking body of work, Ko Un was recently honoured with the 2008 Griffin Poetry Prize Lifetime Recognition Award.

Priscila Uppal (b. 1974) is a Toronto poet, novelist, and professor of English at York University. Among her acclaimed publications are five collections of poetry: *How to Draw Blood From a Stone* (1998), *Confessions of a Fertility Expert* (1999), *Pretending to Die* (2001), *Live Coverage* (2003) and *Ontological Necessities* (2006; shortlisted for the Griffin Poetry Prize); the novels *The Divine Economy of Salvation* (2002), and *To Whom It May Concern* (2009); and a critical study *We Are What We Mourn: The Contemporary English-Canadian Elegy*. Her work has been translated into Dutch, Greek, Korean, Croatian, Latvian, and Italian, and her selected poems, *Successful Tragedies*, is forthcoming from Bloodaxe Books (U.K.) in 2010.

Paul Vermeersch (b. 1973) is the author of three collections of poetry, most recently *Between the Walls* (McClelland & Stewart, 2005). His next collection, *The Reinvention of the Human Hand*, will be published next year. He is also a teacher, editor and occasional book reviewer. He is a dual citizen of both Canada and Belgium and lives in Toronto.

Andrei Voznesensky (b. 1933), born in Moscow, is considered one of Russia's finest twentieth-century poets. His first poems were published in 1958 and readers immediately recognized a unique style, including a complex rhythmical system and sur-real metaphors. In 1978, he was awarded the USSR State Prize. His poetry has been translated into many languages and often by the world's major poets – in English, he has been translated by W.H. Auden, Stanley Kunitz, Richard Wilbur, and more.

Darren Wershler (b. 1966) is the author or co-author of ten books, most recently, *The Iron Whim: A Fragmented History of Typewriting* (McClelland & Stewart, Cornell UP), and *apostrophe* (ECW), with Bill Kennedy. Darren is an Assistant Professor of Communication Studies at Wilfrid Laurier University, and is also part of the faculty at the CFC Media Lab TELUS Inter-active Art & Entertainment Program.

Ko Un's poems by permission of the author (from *Poems Left Behind* or *Poems I Left Behind* in English).

ACKNOWLEDGEMENTS

Thank you to all participating poets, including translating and translated poets, as well as estates, for your generosity and enthusiasm for this project, for working *pro bono* and for waiving fees. All proceeds will go towards funding the publication of poetry translations.

Thank you, as well, to research assistants Jennifer Hann, Winona McMorrow, and Christina Sacchetti. Thank you to Ray Ellenwood for helping to compile the appendices. Thank you to Gabriela Campos, Dae-Tong Huh, Sandra Huh, Vivian Ralickas, Barbara Zolf, and others for foreign language assistance.

Thank you to Barry Callaghan, Michael Callaghan, Nina Callaghan, and everyone at Exile Editions for supporting this project. Thank you, in particular, to Richard Teleky, for much encouragement.

Lastly, thank you to Christopher Doda, for living with me over many centuries and in so many languages.

APPENDIX A
Book-length Translations by Exile Editions

Amichai, Yehuda and Ritsos, Yannis. (Hebrew, Greek.) *Amichai and Ritsos: Two Long Poems, "Travels of a Latter-day Benjamin of Tudela" and "Helen".* trans. Ruth Nevo (Amichai) and Nikos and Gwendolyn Tsingos (Ritsos), 1976. English and Hebrew, facing pages.

Amichai, Yehuda. (Hebrew, Israeli.) *Travels: a Bilingual Edition*, trans. Ruth Nevo, 1986. Hebrew and English, facing pages. (Republished 2001, Picas Series.)

Archambault Theatre Group. (Québécois.) *No Big Deal!*, trans. David Homel, 1982.

Aristophanes. (Ancient Greek.) *The Birds, after the play of Aristophanes*, treans. Gwendolyn MacEwen, 1993.

Aude. (Québécoise.) *Human*, trans. Nora Alleyn, 2006.

_____. *The Indiscernible Movement*, trans. Jill Cairns, 1998.

_____. *The Whole Man*, trans. Jill Cairns, 2000.

Beaulieu, Michel. (Québécois.) *Countenances*, poems, trans. Josée Michaud, 1986.

_____. *Kaleidoscope: Perils of a Solelmn Body*, trans. Arlette Francière, 1998.

_____. *Perils of a Solemn Body*, poems, trans. Arlette Francière, 1988.

_____. *Spells of Fury/ Charmes de la Fureur*, trans. Arlette Francière, 1984. French and English, facing pages. (Republished 2003, Picas Series.)

Beaulieu, Victor-Lévy. (Québécois.) *Jos Connaissant, A Novel*, trans. Ray Chamberlain, 1982.

_____. *A Québécois Dream*, trans. Ray Chamberlain, 1978.

_____. *Satan Belhumeur*, trans. Ray Chamberlain, 1983.

_____. *Steven Le Hérault*, trans. Ray Chamberlain, 1987.

Bessette, Gérard. (Québécois.) *The Cycle*, trans. A.D. Martin-Sperry, 1987.

_____. *Incubation, a Novel*, trans. Glen Shortliffe. 1986.

_____. *Not for Every Eye*, trans. Glen Shortlifffe, 1984. (Republished 1994, Picas Series.)

Blais, Marie-Claire. (Québécoise.) *A Season in the Life of Emmanuel*, trans. Derek Coltman, introduction by Priscila Uppal, 2008. Exile Classics Series.

_____. *Anna's World*, trans., trans. Sheila Fischman, introduction by Camilla Gibb, 2009. Exile Classics Series.

_____. *Deaf to the City*, trans. Carol Dunlop, introduction by Richard Teleky, 2006. Exile Classics Series.

_____. *Nights in the Underground*, trans. Ray Ellenwood, drawings by Mary Meigs, introduction by Janice Kulyk Keefer, 2006. Exile Classics Series.

_____. *The Ocean*, a play, trans. Ray Chamberlain, 1977.

_____. *The Wolf*, trans. Sheila Fischman, introduction by Shyam Selvadurai, 2008. Exile Classics Series.

_____, and Mary Meigs. *Illustrations for Two Novels by Marie-Claire Blais*, illustrations by Mary Meigs, text by Marie-Claire Blais, French and English bilingual edition, 1977.

Borduas, Paul-Emile et al. (Québécois.) *Refus global/Total Refusal*, manifesto, trans. Ray Ellenwood, 1985. (Republished 1998.)

Böszörményi, Zoltán. (Hungarian.) *Far From Nothing*, novel, trans. Paul Sohar, 2006.

Brault, Jacques. (Québécois.) *Fragile Moments*, trans. Barry Callaghan, 1985. French and English, facing pages. (Republished 2000, Picas Series.)

_____. *On the Road No More*, trans. David Sobelman, 1993. French and English, facing pages.

Cavalli, Patrizia. (Italian.) *My Poems Will Not Change the World: Selected Poems 1974-1992*, trans. Judith Baumel, Dina Boni, Barry Callaghan, Patrizia Cavalli, Mario Fazzini, Paulo Fietta, Kenneth Koch, Robert McCracken, Francesca Valente, Christopher Whyte, 1998. Italian and English, facing pages.

Dé, Claire. (Québécoise.) *Desire as Natural Disaster*, trans. Lazer Lederhendler, 1995.

_____. *The Sparrow Has Cut the Day in Half*, trans. Lazer Lederhendler, 1998.

_____. *Soundless Loves*, trans. Lazer Lederhendler, 1996.

Delius, Friedrich Christian. (German.) *The Pears of Ribbeck,* trans. Hans Werner, 1991.

Drach, Ivan. (Ukrainian). *The Madonna of Chernobyl and Other Poems*, trans. Mark Rudman, 1989.

_____. *Orchard Lamps*, ed. Stanley Kunitz, various translators, with woodcuts by Jacques Hnizdovsky, 1989.

Ducharme, Réjean. (Québécois.) *Ha! Ha!* trans. David Homel, 1986.

Euripides, and Yannis Ritsos. (Ancient Greek and Modern Greek.) *The Trojan Women, Helen, and Orestes*, trans. Gwendolyn MacEwen and Nikos Tsingos, 1990.

Ferron, Jacques. (Québécois.) *The Cart*, trans. Ray Ellenwood, 1980. (Republished 1988).

_____. *Papa Boss/Quince Jam/Credit Due*, prose texts, trans. Ray Ellenwood, 1992.

_____. *The Penniless Redeemer*, trans. Ray Ellenwood, 1984.

Gauvreau, Claude. (Québécois.) *The Charge of the Expormidable Moose*, play, translated by Ray Ellenwood, 1996.

_____. *Entrails*, trans. Ray Ellenwood, 1991.

Giguère, Roland. (Québécois.) *Rose and Thorn: Selected Poems*, trans. Donald Winkler, 1988.

Hénault, Gilles. (Québécois.) *Signals for Seers*, poems, trans. Ray Ellenwood, 1988. (Republished 2000, Picas Series.)

Holoborodko, Vasyl. (Ukrainian.) *Icarus with Butterfly Wings and Other Poems*, trans. Myrosia Stefaniuk, 1991.

Hungarian Short Stories, ed. Paul Varnai, various translators, 1983.

Incontro: Where Italy and Canada Meet: Photographs by John Reeves, introduction by Francesca Valente, various translators of the Italian texts, 1996.

Italville: New Italian Writing, ed. Lorenzo Pavolini, various translators, 2005.

Kalynets, Ihor. (Ukrainian.) *Crowning the Scarecrow*, trans. Marco Carynnyk, 1990. Ukrainian and English, facing pages.

Lapointe, Paul-Marie. (Québécois.) *The 5th Season*, trans. D. G. Jones, 1985.

Lords of Winter and of Love: A Book of Canadian Love Poems in English and French, ed. Barry Callaghan, various translators, 1983.

Marteau, Robert. (French.) *Atlante*, trans. Barry Callaghan, 1979. French and English, facing   pages.

_____. *Eidolon*, trans. Barry Callaghan, 1990. Reprints of *Treatise on White and Tincture* and *Atlante*. English and French, facing pages.

_____. *Interlude*, trans. Barry Callaghan, 1982.

_____. *Mount Royal*, novel, trans. David Homel, 1982.

_____. *Pentecost*, novel, trans. David Ellis, 1979.

_____. *Pig-skinning*, novella, trans. David Homel, 1984. (Republished 2006, Picas Series).

_____. *River Without End: A Logbook of the Saint Lawrence*, trans. David Homel, 1987.

_____. *Traité du blanc et des teintures/Treatise on White and Tincture*, trans. Barry Callaghan, 1979. French and English, facing pages.

_____. *Venise en miroir/Venice at Her Mirror*, poetic text, trans. Alexandre Amprimoz, 1991.

_____. *Voyage to Vendée*, trans. David Homel, 1987.

Mihalić, Slavko. (Croatian.) *Black Apples: Selected Poems 1954-1987*, trans. Bernard Johnson, 1989. Croatian and English, facing pages.

Morency, Pierre. (Québécois.) *The Eye Is an Eagle*, trans. Linda Gaboriau, 1992.

_____. *A Season for Birds*, trans. Alexandre Amprimoz, 1990. French and English, facing pages.

Nepveu, Pierre. (Québécois.) *Romans-fleuves*, trans. Donald Winkler, 1998.

Neruda, Pablo. (Spanish, Chilean.) *100 Love Sonnets*, trans. Gustavo Escobedo, Introduction by Rosemary Sullivan, paintings by Gabriela Campos, 2004. Spanish and English, facing pages. (Republished 2007, Exile Classics Series.)

Ouellette, Fernand. (Québécois.) *Wells of Light*, trans. Barry Callaghan and Ray Ellenwood, 1989. (Republished 2003, Picas Series.)

Pasolini, Pier Paolo. (Italian.) *Poetry*, selected and translated by Antonino Mazza, 1991.

Pasternak, Boris. (Russian.) *My Sister-life*, poems, trans. Mark Rudman with Bohdan Boychuk, 1989.

Pavlović, Miodrag. (Serbian.) *Kaphke/Links,* trans. Bernard Johnson, 1989. Serbian and English, facing pages.

_____. *Singing at the Whirlpool*, trans. Barry Callaghan, 1983. Serbian and English, facing pages.

_____. *A Voice Locked in Stone*, trans. Barry Callaghan, 1985. Serbian and English, facing pages.

Pelchat, Jean. (Québécois.) *The Afterlife of Vincent Van Gogh*, trans. Lazer Lederhendler, 2001.

Riel, Louis. (Québécois.) *Selected Poetry of Louis Riel*, trans. Paul Savoie, 1993. French and English, facing pages. (Republished 2000, Picas Series.)

Sabines, Jaime. (Spanish, Mexican.) *Weekly Diary and Poems in Prose & Adam and Eve Poems*, trans. Colin Carberry, 2004. Spanish and English, facing pages.

Salivarová, Zdena. (Czech.) *Ashes, Ashes, All Fall Down*, trans. Jan Drábek, 2000. Picas Series.

Schäedlich, Hans Joachim. (German.) *Eastwestberlin,* trans. Hans Werner, 1992.

Simonsuuri, Kirsti. (Finnish.) *Boy Devil*, novel, trans. by Seija Paddon, 1992.

Slaviček, Milivoj. (Croatian.) *Silent Doors*, trans. Branko Gorjup and Jeanette Lynes, 1988. Croatian and English, facing pages.

Šoljan, Antun. (Croatian.) *The Stone Thrower and Other Poems*, trans. Charles Simic, A.S. Tomson, A. Nizeteo, G. Marvin Tatum, A.R. Mortimer, Bernard Johnson, 1990. Croatian and English, facing pages.

Tremblay, Michel. (Québécois.) *The Guid Sisters*, trans. William Findlay and Martin Bowman, 1988. Translation of the Québécois joual play *Les Belles Soeurs* into modern Scots. (Republished 2000, Picas Series.)

Ungaretti, Giuseppe. (Italian.) *A Major Selection of the Poetry of Giuseppe Ungaretti*, trans. Diego Bastianutti, 1997. Italian and English, facing pages.

Vorobyov, Mykola. (Ukranian.) *Wild Dog Rose Moon*, trans. Myrosia Stefaniuk, 1992. Ukranian and English, facing pages.

Werup, Jacques. (Swedish.) *The Time in Malmö on the Earth*, trans. Roger Greenwald, 1989.

Zeller, Ludwig. (Spanish, Mexican.) *Totem Women*, trans. Susanna Wald, sculpture by Claire Weissman Wilks, 1993. Spanish and English, facing pages.

Ziedonis, Imants. (Latvian.) *Flowers of Ice*. poems, translated by Barry Callaghan, preface by John Montague, 1987.

Zigaina, Giuseppe. (Italian.) *Passolini Between Enigma and Prophecy*, trans. Jennifer Russell, 1990.

APPENDIX B

Translation in *Exile: The Literary Quarterly*

VOLUME 1, #1 (1972)
— Samar Attar (Arabic, Syrian), "The Return of the Dead," poem trans. by author.
— Yehuda Amichai (Hebrew, Israeli) three short poems, trans. Harold Schimmel.
— Michel Deguy (French), a poem, trans. Serge Fauchereau and John Montague.
— Marie-Claire Blais (Québécoise), second chapter from the novel *Le Loup*, trans. Louise Delisle.

VOLUME 1, #2 (1972)
— Yehia Hakki (Arabic, Egyptian), short story "An Empty Bed," trans. Samar Attar.
— Robert Marteau (French, living in Canada), six poems, trans. John Montague.
— Claude Gauvreau (Québécois), short play, poem, essay, trans. Ray Ellenwood.

VOLUME 1, #3 (1974)
— Roch Carrier (Québécois), "Hunting Les Anglais," trans. Sheila Fischman.
— Jacques Ferron (Québécois), *Papa Boss* (60-page novella), trans. Ray Ellenwood.

VOLUME 1, #4 (1974)
— Françoise Xenakis (French), "She'd Tell him on the Island: A Play for Stereophonic Radio," trans. Margaret Pacsu.
— Philippe Thoby-Marcelin (Haïtian/U.S), four poems, trans. Ray Ellenwood.
— Marie-Claire Blais (Québécoise), from *St. Lawrence Blues*, trans. Ralph Manheim.

VOLUME 2, #1 (1974)
— Yehuda Amichai (Hebrew, Israeli), four poems from the war, trans. by the author.
— Jacques Ferron (Québécois), *Quince Jam*, complete novella, trans. Ray Ellenwood.
— Yannis Ritsos (Greek), trans. Nikos and Gwendolyn (MacEwen) Tsingos.
— Mercè Rodoreda (Catalonian), two stories, trans. David Rosenthal.

Volume 2, #2 (1974)
—No translations.

Volume 2, #3-4 (1975)
— Joyce Mansour (French) *Jules César* (novella), trans. Ray Ellenwood. (also trans. of short texts for Jean Benoît objects).
— Yannis Ritsos (Greek), *Helen*, long poem, trans. Nikos and Gwendolyn Tsingos.

Volume 3, #1 (1975)
— Marie-Claire Blais (Québécoise), "The Testament of Jean-Le-Maigre to his Brothers," draft of part of a novel never published, trans. Ray Ellenwood.
— Yehuda Amichai (Hebrew, Israeli), *The Travels of a Latter-Day Benjamin of Tudela*, long poem, trans. Ruth Nevo.
— Joyce Mansour (French), eight poems, trans. Ray Ellenwood.
— André Frenaud (French), eight poems, trans. Evelyn Robson and John Montague.
— Mercè Rodoreda (Catalonian), "A Letter," trans. David Rosenthal.

Volume 3, #2 (1976)
— Jacques Ferron (Québécois), three stories, trans. Betty Bednarski; and "Claude Gauvreau" trans. Ray Ellenwood.
— Claude Gauvreau (Québécois), "Ode to the Enemy" and "Three Dramatic Objects," trans. Ray Ellenwood.
— Philippe Jaccottet (French) three poems, trans. John Montague.
— Jaime Gil de Biedma (Spanish), four poems, trans. Elaine Kerrigan.

Volume 3, #3-4 (1976)
— Réjean Ducharme (Québécois), "The Zone of Hardy Deciduous Forests" from *L'Hiver de Force*, trans. Ray Chamberlain.
— Yannis Ritsos (Greek), *Orestes*, trans. Nikos Tsingos and Gwendolyn Tsingos.
— Pierre Jean Jouve (French), three poems, trans. John Montague.

Volume 4, #1 (1976)
—Breyten Breytenbach (Afrikaans, South Africa), ten poems plus "Vulture Culture," poems and non-fiction piece trans. by André Brink.
— France Théoret (Québécoise), "The Sampler," trans. David Ellis.
— Nicole Brossard (Québécoise), "The Writer," trans. David Ellis.
— Marie-Claire Blais (Québécoise), "Marcelle," trans. David Ellis.

VOLUME 4, #2 (1977)
— Yehuda Amichai (Hebrew, Israeli), "Seven Laments for the Fallen in the War," trans. by the author and Ted Hughes.
— Jacques Ferron (Québécois), from *The Cart*, trans. Ray Ellenwood.
— André Frenaud (French), sixteen poems, trans. John Montague and Evelyn Robson.
— Paul Celan (German), eighteen poems, trans. Michael Hamburger.

VOLUME 4, #3-4 (1977)
— Marie-Claire Blais (Québécoise), *The Ocean*, play, trans. Ray Chamberlain.
— Robert Marteau (French), from *Pentecost: A Novel*, trans. David Ellis.

VOLUME 5, #1-2 (1977)
— Roch Carrier (Québécois), Part 1 of *The Garden of Earthly Delights*, trans. Sheila Fischman.
— Robert Marteau (French), from *Atlante*, trans. Barry Callaghan.
— Jaime Gil de Biedma (Spanish), four poems, trans. Anthony Kerrigan.

VOLUME 5, #3-4 (1978)
— Claude Estaban (French), "Transparent God," poems, trans. John Montague and Evelyn Robson.
— Jacques Ferron (Québécois), "La Sorgne," trans. Ray Ellenwood.
— Robert Marteau (French), from *Atlante*, trans. Barry Callaghan.
— Marie-Claire Blais (Québécoise), from *Nights in the Underground*, trans. Ray Ellenwood.
— Guillevic (French), "Carmac," poem, trans. John Montague.
— Victor-Lévy Beaulieu (Québécois), from *A Québécois Dream*, trans. Ray Chamberlain.

VOLUME 6, #1-2 (1979)
— No translations.

VOLUME 6, #3-4 (1979)
— Robert Marteau, from *Treatise on Tincture and White*, trans. Barry Callaghan.

VOLUME 7, #1-2 (1980)
— Réjean Ducharme (Québécois), from *Bittersea*, trans. David Homel.
— Louis Goulet (Manitoba Métis), "She Wins," trans. Ray Ellenwood.
— Archambault Theatre Collective (Québécois), "Scenes of Maximum Security," from *It Don't Mean Nothing*, trans. Ray Chamberlain and Ray Ellenwood.

VOLUME 7, #3-4 (1981)
— Raymond Queneau (French), "Exercises in Style," trans. M.B. Thompson.
— Jacques Ferron (Québécois), from *The Cart*, trans. Ray Ellenwood.
— Claude Gauvreau (Québécois), four plays, trans. Ray Ellenwood.
— Marie-Claire Blais (Québécoise), from *Deaf to the City*, trans. Carol Dunlop.

VOLUME 8, #1-2 (1981)
— Victor-Lévy Beaulieu (Québécois), from *Jos Connaissant*, trans. Ray Chamberlain.
— Italo Calvino (Italian), from *If on a Winter's Night a Traveller*, trans. William Weaver (name not given in magazine).
— Stéphane Mallarmé (French), "The Afternoon of a Fawn: Eclogue," trans. Marc Widershien.
— Jaroslav Hasek (Czech), *The Red Commissar*, trans. Sir Cecil Parrott.
— Michel Beaulieu (Québécois), from *Spells of Fury*, poems, trans. Arlette Francière.

VOLUME 8, #3-4 (1981)
— Yehuda Amichai (Hebrew, Israeli), "Great Tranquility: Questions and Answers," poems, trans. Tudor Parfit and Glenda Abramson.
—Aharon Appelfeld (Hebrew, Israeli), from *The Age of Wonders*, novel, trans. not listed.
— Miodrag Pavlović (Serbian), "Singing at the Whirlpool," poems, trans. Barry Callaghan.

VOLUME 9, #1 (1982)
— Gyorgy Moldova (Hungarian), "The Sixth Book of Moses," trans. Thomas and Marietta Morry.
— Robert Marteau (French), "Interlude," trans. Barry Callaghan.
— Istvan Csurka (Hungarian), "Happening," trans. Nicholas Rand.
— Joseph Skvorecky (Czech), "Oh, Maytime Witch!," trans. Paul Wilson.

VOLUME 9, #2-4 (1984)
— Victor-Lévy Beaulieu (Québécois), from *Satan Belhumeur*, trans. Ray Chamberlain.
— Miodrag Pavlović (Serbian), *A Voice Locked in Stone*, poems, trans. Barry Callaghan.
— Jacques Ferron (Québécois), from *The Penniless Redeemer*, trans. Ray Ellenwood.
— Nicole Brossard (Québécoise), from *Lovhers*, poems, trans. Barbara Godard.

— Michel Beaulieu (Québécois), from *Semblances*, poems, trans. Josée Michaud.

VOLUME 10, #1 (1985)
— Jacques Brault (Québécois), from *Fragile Moments*, poems, trans. Barry Callaghan.
— Miodrag Bulatovic (Serbian), "Stop the Danube," trans. Srdjan Bogosavljevic.
— Denis Vanier (Québécois), "Acid Lesbians," poems, trans. Barry Callaghan.
— Miroslav Josic Visnjic (Serbian), "Chaste Helen," trans. Sanja Gligorijevic.
— Radoslav Bratic (Serbian), "A Picture Without Father," trans. Krinstina Pribicevic.
— Gérald Godin (Québécois), "Kébékanto of Love," poem, trans. Barry Callaghan.

VOLUME 10, #2 (1985)
— Gilles Hénault (Québécois), five poems, trans. Ray Ellenwood.
— Fernand Ouellette (Québécois), seven poems, trans. Barry Callaghan.
— Michel Beaulieu (Québécois), "The Blues," poem, trans. Barry Callaghan.
— Renaud Lonchamps (French), from *Eighty Evolutionary Propositions: Quaternary*, poem, trans. Barry Callaghan.
— Pierre Morency (Québécois), two poems, trans. Barry Callaghan.

VOLUME 10, #3-4 (1985)
— Imants Ziedonis (Latvian), six poems, trans. not credited, but by Barry Callaghan.
— Alejandra Pizarnik (Argentinian), "The Bloody Countess," trans. Alberto Manguel.
— Michel Beaulieu (Québécois), from *Snow*, poems, trans. Josée Michaud.
— Gérard Bessette (Québécois), from *The Cycle*, trans. A.D. Martin-Sperry.
— Joyce Mansour (French), seven poems, trans. Ray Ellenwood.

VOLUME 11, #1 (1985)
—Réjèan Ducharme (Québécois), from *Ha! Ha!*, play, trans. David Homel.
—Lars Forsell (Swedish), from *Nijinsky*, suite of poems, trans. Jay Lutz.
—Imants Ziedonis (Latvian) from *Meditations on Milk,* poems, trans. Barry Callaghan.
—Katarina Frostenson (Swedish), six poems, trans. Roger Greenwald.

VOLUME 11, #2 (1986)
—Marie-Claire Blais (Québécoise), "Tenderness," short story, trans. Luise von Flotow-Evans.

VOLUME 11, #3 (1986)
—George Trakle (German), eleven poems, trans. Robin Skelton.
—Victor-Lévy Beaulieu (Québécois), from *Steven Le Herault*, novel, trans. Ray Chamberlain.
—Anne Dandurand (Québécoise), "The Inside Killer," short story, trans. Luise von Flotow-Evans.
—Dragan Dragojlović (Serbian), from *Mare's Tail Tea*, poems, trans. Bernard Johnson.

VOLUME 11, #4 (1987)
—Ma Gao Ming (Chinese), three poems, trans. by author and Shirley Kaufman.
—Robert Marteau (French), from *River Without End: A Logbook of the Saint Lawrence*, novel, trans. David Homel.
—Jacques Werup (Swedish), seven poems, trans. Roger Greenwald.
—Nuala Ni Dhomnaill (Irish), six poems, trans. Michael Harnett, John Montague, and Paul Muldoon.
—Roland Giguère (Québécois), "Rose and Thorn," poem, trans. Donald Winkler.
—Claire Dé (Québécois), "It Would Be Night," short story, trans. Luise von Flotow-Evans.

VOLUME 12, #1 (1987)
—Abraham Sutskever (Yiddish), "Green Aquarium," short story, trans. Seymour Levitan.
—Boris Pasternak (Russian), "The Subline Malady," poem, trans. Mark Rudman.
—Nicole Brossard (Québécoise), "Aroused," poem sequence, trans. Alexandre L. Amprimoz.
—Tomas Tranströmer (Swedish), four poems, trans. Göran Malmquist.

VOLUME 12, #2 (1987)
—Yehuda Amichai (Hebrew, Israeli), "To Love in Jerusalem," play, trans. Richard Farber.
—Gérard Bessette (Québécois), from *The Cycle*, novel, trans. A.D. Martin-Sperry.
—Imants Ziedonis (Latvian), from *Flowers of Ice*, prose pieces, trans. Barry Callaghan.

VOLUME 12, #3 (1988)
—Nikola Petković, "The Hoppers," short story, trans. Slobodon Drenovac.
—Tristan Corbière (French), "The Wandering Mistrel and the Pardon of Saint Anne," poem, trans. Peter Dale.

—Robert Marteau (French), "Three Sonnets," trans. Barry Callaghan.
—Jaime Gil de Biedma (Spanish), three poems, trans. Elaine Kerrigan.
—Arie van den Berg (Dutch), *Owls*, poems, trans. Scott Rollins and Peter Nijmeijen.
—Roland Giguère (Québécois), ten poems, from *Rose and Thorn: Selected Poems*, trans. Donald Winkler.
—Gilles Hénault, from *Signals for Seers*, poems, trans. Ray Ellenwood.

VOLUME 12, #4 (1988)
—Yves Theriault (Québécois), Acadian of part Montagnais Indian ancestry), "Missus Anna," short story, trans. Ray Ellenwood.
—Andrei Voznesensky (Russian), from *The Ditch: A Spiritual Proceeding*, poems/prose, trans. Barry Callaghan and Natalia Mayer.
—Aristophanes' *The Birds* (Ancient Greek comedy-drama) adapted by Gwendolyn MacEwen.
—Attilio Bertolucci (Italian), eight poems, trans. Charles Tomlinson.

VOLUME 13, #1 (1988)
—Michel Tremblay (Québécois), from *The Guid Sisters*, play, trans. William Findley and Martin Bowman into modern Scots from the Québécois joual *Les Belles Soeurs*.

VOLUME 13, #2 (1989)
—Mihály Kornis (Hungarian), "Petition," short story, trans. Ivan Sanders.
—Jean Joubert (French), four poems, trans. Hilary Davies.
—Roland Giguère (Québécois), from *Rose and Thorn*, prose poems, trans. Donald Winkler.
—Iván Mándy (Hungarian), "Night of the Sweat-Soaked Shirt," short story, trans. Chris Outtram and Éva Rácz.
—Rita Tornborg (Swedish), "Kajamec," short story, trans. Patricia Campton.

VOLUME 13, #3 (1989)
—Michel Beaulieu (Québécois), *Among Other Cities*, long poem, trans. Arlette Francière.
—Mimmo Morian (Italian), *Seven Solitudes for an Island*, poem sequence, trans. Mark O'Connor.

VOLUME 13, #4 (1989)
—Slavko Mihalić, poem from *Black Apples*, trans. Bernard Johnson.

VOLUME 14, #1 (1989)
—Kazuko Shiraishi (Japanese), four poems, trans. Sally Ito.

VOLUME 14, #2 (1989)
—Ivan Drach (Ukrainian), four poems, trans. Paul Nemser, Mark Rudman, Carol Muske, and Paula Schwartz.
—Charles Baudelaire (French), "The Voyage," poem, trans. Peter Dale.
—Nikola Šop (Croatian), *Cottages in Space*, long poem, trans. Branko Brusar and W.H. Auden.
—Pierre Morency (Québécois), two poems, trans. Alexandre Amprimoz.
—Pier Paolo Pasolini (Italian), two poems, from *Alì Blue-Eyes*, and "Teorema (an Aside)," trans. Antonino Mazza.

VOLUME 14, #3 (1990)
—Gunter Kunert (German), "In the Closet," short story, trans. Hans Werner.
—Milivoj Slaviček (Croatian), four poems, trans. Branko Gorjup and Jeannette Lynes.
—Heinz Piontek (German), "Other Catchwords," short prose, trans. Ken Fontenot.
—Gabriele Eckart (German), "Feldberg and Back," short story, trans. Wayne Kvam.

VOLUME 14, #4 (1990)
—Osman Lins (Portuguese, Brazil), "Pastroral," short story, trans. Adria Frizzi.
—Naguib Mahfouz (Arabic, Egyptian), "The Mosque in the Narrow Lane," short story, trans. Nadia Faraq, revised by Josephine Wahba and Barry Callaghan.

VOLUME 15, #1 (1990)
—Antun Šoljan (Croatian), "Stone Thrower," poem, trans. Charles Simic.
—Pierre Morency (Québécois), "Personal Effects," poem, trans. Alexandre Amprimoz.
—Gunter Kunert (German), "Dreamchild," short story, trans. Hans Werner.
—Ihor Kalynets (Ukrainian), three poems, trans. Marco Carynnyk.

VOLUME 15, #2 (1991)
—Vasyl Holoborodko (Ukrainian), "Katerina (fugue)," poem, trans. Bohdan Boychuk.
—Vasko Popa (Serbian), "Give Me Back My Rags," poem sequence trans. Charles Simic.
—Jude Stéfan (French), six poems, trans. John Montague.

VOLUME 15, #3 (1991)
—No translations.

VOLUME 15, #4 (1991)
—Gaston Miron (Québécois), six poems, trans. Paul Savoie.
—Hans Joachin Schädich (German), *East/West Berlin*, prose, trans. Hans Werner.
—Hélène Dorion (Québécoise), *Out of Focus,* long poem, trans. Andrea Moorhead.
—Friedrich Christian Delius (German), from *The Pears of Ribbeck*, novel, trans. Hans Werner.

VOLUME 16 #1-4 (1992)
—These issues were replaced by *15 Years in Exile Vols 1 and II* (reprinted pieces in English and English translation taken from Exile's first fifteen years), and *Exile's Exiles: The Happy Few* (this volume plus the combined Exile 16.2 and 16.3 volume are photographs of Exile authors and reproductions of their actual handwriting).

VOLUME 17, #1 (1992)
—Ivan Slamnig (Croatian), *Squares of Sorrow*, poems, trans. Milka Lukić.
—Ivana Malenkova (Serbian), *Festivals of Babylon*, poems, trans. Milka Lukić.
—Tomaz Salumun (Slovenian), three poems, trans. Michael Biggins.
—Claire Dé (Québécoise), "A Devouring Love," short story, trans. Sam Leibman.

VOLUME 17, #2 (1993)
—No translations.

VOLUME 17, #3 (1993)
—Francic Ponge (French), three poems, trans. John Montague.

VOLUME 17, #4 (1993)
—Jacques Brault (Québécois), from *On the Road No More*, poems, trans. David Sobelman.

VOLUME 18, #1 (1994)
—No translations.

VOLUME 18, #2 (1994)
—Primo Levi (Italian), twelve poems, trans. M. L. Rosenthal.

VOLUME 18, #3 (1994)
—Rakel Liehu (Finnish), *Cubisms*, poems, trans. Seija Paddon.

—Claire Dé (Québécoise), "Slices of Mealtime," short story, trans. Lazer Lederhendler.

—Giuseppe Ungaretti (Italian), "Day by Day 1940-1946," poem sequence trans. Diego Bastianutti.

VOLUME 18, #4 (1994)

—Tristan Bernard (French), "The Exile," play, unknown trans.

—Armando Pajalich (Italian), "On the 18th Anniversary of P.P. Pasolini's Murder," poem, trans. by author.

—Fluvio Tomizza (Italian), "A Better Life," short story, trans. Francesca Valente.

VOLUME 19, #1 (1995)

—Sappho (Ancient Greek), eight poems, trans. by Anita George.

VOLUME 19, #2 (1995)

—Andrea Zanzotto (Italian), eight poems, trans. Beverly Allen and Gino Rizzo.

VOLUME 19, #3 (1995)

—A.B. Yehoshua (Hebrew, Israeli), "Night Babies," play, trans. Miriam Shlesinger.

VOLUME 19, #4 (1995)

—Hans Sahl (German), four stories, trans. Hans Werner.

VOLUME 20, #1 (1996)

—Gérald Tougas (Québécois), "Fête du Canada Day," short story, trans. Rachelle Renaud.

VOLUME 20, #2 (1996)

—Claire Dé (Québécoise), from *Soundless Loves*, novel, trans. Lazer Lederhendler.

VOLUME 20, #3 (1996)

—Vesna Parun (Croatian), five poems, trans. Branko Gorjup and Jeannette Lynes.

—Slavenka Draculić (Croatian), from novel *The Taste of a Man*, no translator name listed.

VOLUME 20, #4 (1996)

—Gottfried Benn (German), twelve poems, trans. James Lawson.

VOLUME 21, #1 (1997)

—Katarina Frostenson (Swedish), two stories, trans. Joan Tate.

—Wislawa Szymborska (Polish), twelve poems, trans. Marta Zaborska-Quinn.

—Ferida Durakovic, from *Heart of Darkness*, three poems, trans. Amela Simic.

VOLUME 21, #2 (1997)

—Andrea Zanzotto (Italian), from *Going Sewing*, poems, trans. Beverly Allen and Gino Rizzo.

VOLUME 21, #3 (1997)

—Andreï Makine (French, Russian), from *Once Upon the River Love*, novel, trans. from the French by by Geoffrey Strachan.

—Miljenko Jergović (Serbian), two stories, trans. Stela Tomašević.

VOLUME 21, #4 (1998)

—Mirkka Rekola (Finnish), from *Sky on Duty*, eleven poems, trans. Hebert Lomas.

—Pierre Nepveu (Québécois), ten poems, trans. Donald Winkler.

VOLUME 22, #1 (1998)

—Ismail Kadare (Albanian), from *The File on H*, novel, trans. David Bellos.

—Patrizia Cavalli (Italian), eight poems, trans. Judith Baumel, Francesca Valente, Kenneth Koch, and Robert McCracken.

—Réjean Ducharme (Québécois), from *The Daughters of Christopher Columbus*, prose, trans. Will Browning.

VOLUME 22, #2 (1998)

—Claire Dé (Québécoise), from *The Sparrow Has Cut the Day in Half*, novel in verse, trans. Lazer Lederhendler.

—Michel Deguy (French), *A Poleoscope*, long poem, trans. Christopher Elson.

—Aude (Québécoise), "The Indiscernable Movement Called Life," and "The Ferryman," short stories, trans. Jill Cairns.

VOLUME 22, #3 (1998)

—No translations.

VOLUME 22, #4 (1998)

—Yehuda Amichai (Hebrew, Israeli), "Jerusalem Is a Merry-Go-Round," poem, trans. Aloma Halter.

—Pierre Morency (Québécois), *Glimmer on the Mountain*, long poem, trans. Brenda Casey and Elizabeth Hahn.

VOLUME 23, #1 (1999)
  —Ludwig Zeller (Spanish, Mexico & Chile), four poems, trans. A.F. Moritz.
  —David Huerta (Spanish, Mexico), six poems, trans. Mark Schafer.

VOLUME 23, #2 (1999)
  —Mónica Lavin (Spanish, Mexico), "Home Again?" short story, trans. Arturo V. Degade and Barry Callaghan.
  —Pia Pera (Italian), from *Lo's Diary*, novel, trans. Ann Goldstein.

VOLUME 23, #3 (1999)
  —Ryszard Kapuściński (Polish), eight poems, trans. Diana Kuprel and Marek Kusiba.

VOLUME 23, #4 (1999)
  —Zoé Valdés (Spanish, Cuba), from *Be Careful, It's My Heart*, novel, trans. Nadia Benabid.
  —Abilio Estévez (Spanish, Cuba & Mexico), from *The Faithful Dead*, novel, trans. David Frye.

VOLUME 24, #1 (2000)
  —Emmanuel Hocquard (French), *This Story Is Mine: Little Autobiographical Dictionary of Elegy*, prose, trans. Norma Cole.
  —Pablo Neruda (Spanish, Chile), five poems, trans. Don Summerhayes.

VOLUME 24, #2 (2000)
  —Federico Andahazi (Spanish), from *The Merciful Women*, novel, trans. Alberto Manguel.
  —Josef Skvorecky (Czech), from *When Eve Was Naked*, novel, trans. Káča Poláčková-Henley.

VOLUME 24, #3 (2000)
  —Yehuda Amichai (Hebrew, Israeli), selected poems, trans. Tudor Parfit, Glenda Abramson, and Ted Hughes.
  —Carsten Jensen (Danish), from *I Have Seen the World Begin*, novel, trans. Barbara Haveland.

VOLUME 24, #4 (2000)
  —Claudia Solis-Ogarrio (Spanish, Mexico), three poems, trans. by the author.

—Joseph Guglielmi (French), *The But Too White: Fables*, long poem, trans. Norma Cole.

—Raquel (French), *Alba*, prose-art, trans. Norma Cole.

—Jacques Roubaud (French), from *Poèsie: Etcetera: Menage*, prose poetry, trans. Norma Cole.

VOLUME 25, #1 (2001)

—Bernardo Ruiz (Spanish, Mexico), "Queen of Shadows," short story, trans. Gustavo V. Segade.

—Francisco Hinojosa (Spanish, Mexico), "Marian Dosal, Juice Vendor," short story, trans. Gustavo V. Segade.

VOLUME 25, #2 (2001)

—Alexander Halvonik (Slovakian), "Fear," short story, trans. Heather Trebatická.

—Peter Holka (Slovakian), "Love as a Crime," short story, trans. Heather Trebatická.

VOLUME 25, #3 (2001)

—Scipione (Italian), *Poems and Drawings*, trans. Brunella Antomarini and Susan Stewart.

—Dane Zajc (Slovenian), from *Scorpions*, poems, trans. Sonja Kravanja.

VOLUME 25, #4 (2001)

—Jean Pelchat (Québécois), from *The Afterlife*, novel, trans. Lazer Lederhendler.

VOLUME 26, #1 (2002)

—Enrique Serna (Spanish, Mexico), "Self Love," short story, trans. Gustavo V. Segade.

—Jean Pierre Girard (Québécois), "How to Abandon One's Career in 20 Easy Lessons," short story, trans. Rachelle Renaud.

—Günter Grass (German), from poem "In the Egg," trans. Michael Hamburger, with artwork by Susana Wald.

—Anton Hykisch (Slovakian), "Murderers," short story, trans. Peter Petro and Hogg (Barry Callaghan).

VOLUME 26, #2 (2002)

—No translations.

VOLUME 26, #3 (2002)

—Mónica Lavin (Spanish, Mexico), "The Lizard," short story, trans. Reginald Gibbons.

—Helle Helle (Danish), "I Drive Back and Forth," short story, trans. Russell L. Dees.

—Nora Ikstena (Latvian), "Amaryllises," short story, trans. Ilze Klavina-Mueller.

—Arvis Kolmanis (Latvian), "The Drunk Cupid or the Dead God," short story, trans. Vitauts Jaunarājs.

VOLUME 28, #3 (2004) (Eight Danish Authors special feature).
—Helle Helle (Danish), three stories, trans. Russell L. Dees and Barbara J. Haveland.

—Henrik Nordbrandt (Danish), sixteen poems, trans. Alexander Taylor, Henrik Nordbrandt, and Roger Greenwald.

—Simon Frueland (Danish), "The Short Story of My Life," short story, trans. Barbara J. Haveland.

—Pia Juul (Danish), nine poems, trans. Barbara J. Haveland.

—Stig Dalager (Danish), from *The Dream*, play, trans. Lone Thygesen Blecher.

—Pia Tafdrup (Danish), eight poems, trans. Roger Greenwald.

—Jøørgen Gustava Brandt (Danish), five poems, trans. Alexander Taylor.

—Christina Hesselholdt (Danish), from *You, My You*, novel, trans. W. Glyn Jones.

VOLUME 28, #4 (2004)
—Sandra Veronesi (Italian), "A Hundred Little Tottis," short story, trans. Anthony Shugaar.

—Arnaldo Colasant (Italian), "The Lesson," short story, trans. Anthony Shugaar.

—Giosuè Calaciura (Italian), "The Ship," short story, trans. Lawrence Garner.

VOLUME 29, #1 (2005)
—Niccolò Ammaniti (Italian), "Dec 9th," short story, trans. Lawrence Garner.

—Carole David (Québécoise), from *Female*, novel, trans. Nora Alleyn.

—Louise Dupré (Québécoise), from *Voice Over*, prose poems, trans. Antonio D'Alfonso.

—France Théoret (Québécoise), from *Girls Closed In*, novel, trans. Luise von Flotow.

—Nicole Brossard (Québécoise), from *Picture Theory*, novel, trans. Barbara Godard.

VOLUME 29, #2 (2005)
—Yehuda Amichai (Hebrew, Israeli), *The Day Martin Buber Was Buried*, play, trans. Noam Flinker and Burton Raffel.

VOLUME 29, #3 (2005)
—No translations.

VOLUME 29, #4 (2005)
—Ludwig Zeller (Spanish, Mexico), eleven poems, trans. A.F. Moritz.

VOLUME 30, #1 (2006)
—No translations.

VOLUME 30, #2 (2006)
—Paul Bélanger (Québécois), from *Windows and Elsewhere*, poems, trans. Antonio D'Alfonso.
—Gilles Cyr (Québécois), two poems, trans. Patrick Williamson and Yann Lovelock.
—Denise Desaultels (Québécoise), "Memorial to Lou," short story, trans. Daniel Sloate.
—Claudine Bertrand (Québécoise), two poems, trans. Antonio D'Alfonso.
—Jaime Sabines (Spanish, Mexico), from *Night Flight*, poems, trans. Colin Carberry.
—Jean Barbe (Québécois), from *How to Become a Monster*, novel, trans. Patricia Wright.

VOLUME 30, #3 (2006)
—Piera Mattei (Italian), "North," short story, trans. by Adrian Cook.

VOLUME 30, #4 (2007; Special 120th Issue – 30th Anniversary Issue)
—Marie-Claire Blais (Québécoise), from *Augustino and the Choir of Destruction*, novel, trans. Nigel Spencer.
—Gonçalo M. Tavares (Portuguese), *Mr. Brecht*, prose poems, trans. Desirée Jung.

VOLUME 31, #1 (2007)
—Michel Duguy (France), "Homage to Hogg," poem, trans. Christopher Elson.
—Horace (Latin), three poems, trans. Ewan Whyte.

VOLUME 31, #2 (2007)
—Zofia Nałkowska (Polish), from *Medallions*, four short stories, trans. Diana Kuprel.
—Thérèse Renaud (Québecoise), from *The Sands of Dream*, poems, trans. Ray Ellenwood.

VOLUME 31, #3 (2007)
—Claire Dé (Québecoise), "Lesley Chadwick," short story, trans. Claire Dé.
—Tomas Tranströmer (Swedish), five poems, trans. Michael McGriff with Mikaela Grassl.
—Anne Dandurand (Québecoise), "A Hand in the Tree (1959)," short story, trans. Rosana Roth.
—Kurt Marti (Bernese Swiss, Switzerland), six poems, trans. Jeff Kochan.

VOLUME 31, #4 (2007)
—Guido Conti (Italian), "The Crocodile Over the Alter," short story, trans. Lawrence Garner.
—Arnaldo Colasanti (Italian), "The Lesson," short story, trans. Anthony Shugaar.

VOLUME 32, #1 (2008)
—Niels Hav, (Danish) two poems, trans. P.K. Brask and Heather Spears.

VOLUME 32, #2 (2008)
—No translations.

VOLUME 32, #3 (2008)
—Carlos Castro Saavedra (Spanish, Colombia), four poems, trans. Hardie St. Martin.

VOLUME 32, #4 (2008)
—José Ramón Heredia (Spanish, Venezulean), five poems, trans. Hardie St. Martin.
—Claude Gauvreau (Québécoise), A Homophonic Translation of Claude Gauvreau's "Trustful Fatigue and Reality," trans. Stephen Cain.

This book is entirely printed on FSC certified paper.